Come Alive

Come Alive

Your Six-point Plan for Lasting Health and Energy

Beth MacEoin

Hodder & Stoughton
LONDON SYDNEY AUCKLAND

Copyright © 2000 by Beth MacEoin

First published in Great Britain in 2000

The right of Beth MacEoin to be identified as
the Author of the Work has been asserted by her in accordance
with the Copyright, Designs and Patents Act 1988.

10 9 8 7 6 5 4

British Library Cataloguing in Publication Data
A record for this book is available from the British Library

ISBN 0 340 74582 7

Typeset by Avon Dataset Ltd, Bidford-on-Avon, Warks

Printed and bound in Great Britain by
The Guernsey Press Co. Ltd, Channel Isles

Hodder & Stoughton
A Division of Hodder Headline Ltd
338 Euston Road
London NW1 3BH

For Denis, who makes it all worthwhile

Contents

Acknowledgements

During the course of writing this book, I have been indebted to the following people who have provided an invaluable amount of inspiration, advice and encouragement. The initial idea for this book came from my editor, Judith Longman, who has been a delight to work with from the start of this project to its end. As always, my agent, Teresa Chris, has been an endless source of good-humoured support. I am also very grateful to those who have given their time so generously in offering advice on specific areas of this book. My warmest thanks are due to Roger Groos, Dr Anand, Swami Satchinanda Ma and Denny Gibson. As always, I have had immense support from my husband, Denis, who gives unstintingly of his time in discussing ideas, reading the latest version of the text, sorting out the mysteries of how to use a computer, making me laugh at grim moments with his Eric Cartman impersonations, and providing essential cups of tea. I must also thnk my mother, Nancy, for providing an essential role model and shaping my vision of what true vitality can be. Finally, my love and thanks to Samantha just for being who she is.

Introduction

Welcome to the six-point plan. In the following pages you will discover how to improve your potential for maximum experience of mental, emotional and physical health. Don't worry, this does not involve adopting an impossibly strict regime that means we have to kiss goodbye to all the indulgences that make life enjoyable and fun. After all, a truly holistic approach to health promotion must take into account that our lives need to retain their full quota of sensual pleasures. On the other hand, the six-point plan isn't so full of compromise that it has little to offer us in terms of positive change. The beauty of the information that follows is that it is flexible enough to be adapted to the busiest of lives and can be taken at whatever pace and order our individual needs dictate.

What is maximum health?

Maximum health is much, much more than not being ill. When we experience optimum health, we should be amazed at how much energy we have, how emotionally balanced we feel and how much better we cope with life in general. Many of us will have known what it feels like to be in this enviable position at some stage in our lives, but we may have gradually lost touch with this feeling as we react to the stresses and pressures of life.

Because the descent into a state of compromised vitality tends to be subtle and insidious, many of us may put up with it for so long that we begin to feel that this is all we can realistically expect. We may also have an unpleasant sense of being overwhelmed by the prospect of making any changes, because we just don't know where on earth to start. As a result, many of us feel so demoralised that we take temporary refuge in another bar of chocolate, an extra couple of glasses of wine, or a cigarette. We make the mistake of putting up with just getting by, instead of realising that we have basic measures at our disposal to help put the zest back into our lives. These make up the framework of the six-point plan.

What this means in terms of manageable commitment

It helps enormously at the outset if we can keep realistic goals in mind when we set about making positive changes in our lives in order to boost our levels of well-being and zest for life. In other words, we are setting out to change the broad framework of our lives for the better, rather than tacking on a few 'band-aid' modifications here and there. The latter only give partial results, which tend to give partial satisfaction. On the other hand, if we realistically evaluate the changes we can make in the long term and stick to them, we may be able to make genuinely positive changes to the quality of the vitality we experience on a daily basis.

The secret to making these changes work is very simple: never go for the drastic approach. This always applies, no matter how desperate we may feel about needing to do something quickly in order to retrieve what may seem a terrible state of unfitness. When we go down the drastic route we may initially feel excited that we are at last doing something about a situation that may have bothered us for a long time, but after a while the pressures of maintaining extreme changes may increasingly force us to compromise and eventually return to our old habits. This tends to be especially the case with extreme dietary restrictions or over-ambitious exercise plans.

On the other hand, if we understand at the outset that, for the six-point plan to work, we must work in harmony with our personal needs, preferences and professional pressures, it is far more likely to work for us in the long term. In other words, we are taking on board a fundamental adjustment in looking after our own state of health, so that we can introduce positive changes to our lifestyles while gently phasing out the more negative aspects. Because these adjustments may involve modifying long-established habits, we need to introduce the changes slowly and steadily.

As with so many other aspects of life, 'going with the grain' is so much easier and more effortless than trying to force ourselves in a direction that just isn't us. This is why the six-point plan is deliberately not limited to a specific time-scale of days, weeks or months: after all, why settle for a short-term solution when we could enjoy better health and increased vitality for the rest of our lives?

Making it work

In order to get the most out of the six-point plan, we need to start with the basics: a realistic evaluation of the global quality of our energy levels, general experience of health and zest for life. In other words, not simply adding up how many times we fall ill during an average year, but taking account of how genuinely alive we can claim to feel on a day-to-day basis. This is an important way of avoiding the 'band-aid' trap when what we may need is a more general overhaul of our lifestyle.

Could you do with a general fine-tuning to boost your energy levels, increase your resistance to infection, improve the range and quality of what you eat, maximise the amount of physical activity you enjoy and gain greater emotional stability? If so, you will benefit from reading the six-point plan from beginning to end in order to get a broad sense of what is involved. Then return to each section, putting into action the recommendations appropriate to you.

Don't worry about how long this may take; some temperaments can act on their objectives very speedily; for others, it may be months or longer before we feel ready to move on to another area of the plan. Always remember to work at your own pace, giving yourself plenty of time to experiment with new possibilities for change.

The most important thing to bear in mind when you start working with the six-point plan is that it's fine to make mistakes and start again. Going off the rails now and again doesn't mean that we have to give up trying to get it right next time around. The basic flexibility of the six-point plan allows for the fact that we are all human and will have days when we just don't make the best decisions. Always remember that making short-term mistakes will not undo the benefits of following the plan up to now. Just pick up the threads again, see what you have learnt about yourself from the experience and get moving with the next step of the six-point plan.

If, on the other hand, you feel that your base-line level of vitality and well-being is generally pretty good, but there are specific areas of your experience of health that could do with some attention, you should focus specifically on the chapters that deal with these issues. You may also want to read some of the other general sections just out of interest, but this is not essential, because each chapter is a complete section in its own right as well as part of a greater whole.

How to set about assessing our lives: immediate and longer-term goals

The easiest way of establishing which is our most pressing health problem is to ask ourselves which aspects of our health most cramp our style. We may have felt limited for ages by lack of energy and physical stamina, panic attacks, recurrent infections, weight problems, or just a general lack of motivation. If these problems have been present for a long time, we should regard them as chronic disorders that can be effectively eliminated by long-term strategies.

It helps to bear in mind that the word 'chronic' doesn't necessarily mean that a condition is especially severe (although it may seem to be); it usually means that a problem is well-established and has a tendency to recur at frequent intervals. As a rule, chronic conditions do not clear up of their own accord. Improvement requires specific action through alternative or conventional medical help, or positive changes in lifestyle.

If a health problem seems very severe or persistent, you may find it very helpful to consult an alternative practitioner in addition to implementing the six-point plan on a broad basis. If you are unsure whether this may be appropriate to you, see the questions on p. 14 of Chapter One 'Energy Boosters'. The information in the six-point plan is designed to complement any advice likely to be given by an alternative practitioner, and so avoid any potential conflict.

On the other hand, if your general levels of health and vitality are very good, but you know you are less physically fit than you should be, or have occasional bouts of feeling negative, you could benefit greatly from concentrating on the information in Chapters Four or Five 'Exercise Boosters' and 'Emotional Boosters'. These are also long-term aims and objectives which need to be incorporated into our lives on an on-going basis.

Areas of our health which will respond to more short-term action include acute problems. These conditions tend to arise abruptly within the context of general good health and often clear up of their own accord, given the right conditions. Good examples of acute problems include an upset stomach, cold, cough, temporary insomnia, short-term anxiety, sore throat, or a headache. Generally, these conditions can be found in Chapter Six 'Quick-fix Boosters' at the end of the book; the basic advice in each section will speed you through any of these problems in double-quick time.

Whatever your ultimate goal in adopting the six-point plan, always remember that half the fun of any journey is the process of travelling, as well as the pleasure of reaching the final destination. I wish you the best of health, happiness and vitality on your voyage to maximum health.

1

Energy Boosters

Energy is one of the fundamental mysteries of life. We can't touch, feel, or smell it, and yet, it is the animating force that tells us we are alive. When our energy levels are flowing at their optimum level we feel confident, positive, and creative. When we feel strong and energised stressful situations appear as challenges rather than threats, ideas come readily and without enormous strain or effort, and we feel we can roll with whatever punches life may throw at us.

Steadily-flowing energy is also essential to support our bodies in the basic processes of maintenance, repair and renewal. When our energy levels are flagging, we fight off illness less effectively and speedily, and life generally loses its sparkle and excitement. In fact, it could be said that we only feel truly alive when our energy levels are at their peak.

Yet it is astonishing how many of us put up with flagging energy levels, largely because we don't know what to do about it. We can be also hampered by the inheritance of the conventional medical model, which tends not to take our energy levels into account when assessing our state of health or illness. As a result, if we are not suffering from a diagnosable condition we often do not question how positively alive and well we feel.

The importance of balance

Is it possible to have too much energy? Most of us would probably claim that we could do with more, but what we should be aiming for in the search for optimum health is balanced rather than excessive energy release. When our energy levels flow smoothly, we have more than enough vitality to accomplish all we need during the day and are also sufficiently relaxed at night to switch off easily. This is in marked contrast to those of us whose energy levels feel so sluggish that we seem to be wading through treacle during the day, or who feel so hyped-up at work that we concentrate badly, and then find ourselves stressed out and wakeful at night.

When our energy levels are flowing consistently we should not hit phases during the day when we suddenly run out of steam, like a car that unexpectedly runs out of petrol. One of the best ways of avoiding this irritating problem is to identify the pattern of our individual energy fluctuations during the day.

Coming clean: Honest assessment of our daily experience of essential energy

Common patterns may include any of the following:

- Wide awake on rising with a mid-morning energy dip around 11 am.
- Raring to go all morning with problems in keeping up the pace after lunch around 2 pm.
- Very sluggish on waking, with energy levels rising to a peak until 3–4 pm, when they rapidly take a dip until mid-evening (around

7–8 pm). There may then be a 'second wind' of vitality and feeling full of energy until bed-time.

- Fine all day until collapsing after work in the early evening around 6 pm. From here until bed-time it is likely to be downhill all the way.
- Exhausted after sleep with a steady improvement as the day goes on. With this sort of pattern, falling asleep at any time of the day can be followed by a slump in energy and feeling sluggish, so that even a brief nap can cause problems.

Of course, there are other possible variations around these themes, with some patterns combining more than one permutation. But these may give us some clues about identifying our own energy patterns through the day.

Initial solutions to energy dips

In this chapter we shall investigate in detail some fundamental ways of improving our levels of energy and zest for life. However, rather than jumping in at the deep end, we shall start with some practical suggestions for change which are immediately accessible. When we see positive results from these adjustments, we shall then have the enthusiasm, interest, and confidence to take on board more radical and far-reaching changes.

The mid-morning slump

If you recognise yourself as regularly running out of fuel between breakfast and lunch, the following simple steps may provide a short-term solution:

- Never be tempted to dash out without having a simple breakfast, otherwise you will be far more likely to run out of steam mid-morning.

- Avoid breakfasts that include large helpings of sugar and caffeine, because these will only temporarily recharge your energy batteries. Instead, opt for wholemeal toast, muesli without refined sugar, fruit juice and caffeine-free beverages such as herbal teas or cereal-based coffee substitutes.

- Above all, avoid heavy and indigestible items such as the traditional British breakfast of bacon, fried bread and sausages. Even when grilled rather than fried, this sort of meal takes ages to digest and can make us feel heavy and sleepy when we need to be alert.

- If you feel empty and hungry around mid-morning, snack on fresh or dried fruit, or a small salad sandwich made with wholemeal bread. At all costs, avoid the trap of grabbing a coffee and a bar of chocolate to keep you going, since this is likely to result in a larger dip in energy further down the line.

The after-lunch slump

- Never be tempted to skip lunch in an attempt to get more work done; this is likely to lead to fuzzy-headedness and exhaustion by early afternoon.

- The optimum lunch should be flavourful, nutritious and light enough not to make you feel you want to curl up and go to sleep afterwards. Try sandwiches made from wholemeal bread with fillings such as tuna, fresh vegetables (roasted or chopped and grated as salad ingredients), chicken, fresh salmon, or hummus. Salads could include grains such as brown rice or couscous as well as a wide range of raw ingredients including avocado, nuts, seeds, and a little low-fat cheese. Steer clear of creamy sauces, mayonnaise and full-fat ingredients such as soft cheese, pasties, pastries and cream.

- Always avoid having alcohol at lunch if you know that you have a tendency to doze in the early afternoon. If fruit juice isn't appealing, opt for one of the non-alcoholic, carbonated, caffeine-free herbal drinks that are increasingly available.

- If you work in an air-conditioned, centrally-heated environment, make sure that you take a short walk in the fresh air at lunch-time in order to blow the cobwebs away. Don't be put off by thinking you don't have time, just a walk around the block and back is usually enough.

The tea-time slump

- Since this usually happens when we are on the last lap of our working day, if you know that you have a vulnerable spot at this time in the afternoon, pace yourself through the earlier part of the day. By adopting this simple strategy you shouldn't have to face a mountain of work put off from the morning when you feel at your lowest.
- Make sure that you have a mid-afternoon break when you can enjoy a piece of fresh fruit and a drink.
- If energy levels are particularly flagging, try a stimulating beverage that contains guarana (provided you don't have a problem with caffeine addiction).
- Try a few cycles of alternate nostril breathing to clear your head and revitalise yourself (see p. 182 for advice on how to practise this technique).
- If you know late afternoon is a time when you often feel exhausted, make a point of not drinking coffee after lunch. Although it initially acts as a stimulant, once the effect has worn off later in the afternoon it can leave us mentally fatigued and craving for more.

The early-evening slump

- Above all else, try to avoid the tempting trap of collapsing in front of the television with a snack and a drink, because you will probably fall asleep shortly afterwards.
- In the spring and summer months, make a point of having a short walk in the fresh air before dinner; this can go a long way towards preventing the exhaustion that can set in at this time of the day.
- On winter nights, opt instead for doing fifteen or twenty minutes

of yoga, using one of the many video tapes available. This is an excellent way of winding down from a stressful day and revitalising yourself for the evening ahead.

- If you are planning an evening out, take an energising shower with an aromatherapy-based shower gel that includes invigorating citrus essential oils. On the other hand, if you are at home for the evening and less pressed for time, take a long refreshing bath with the same essential oils.

The energy slump after waking

- Feeling awful on waking can be related to poor quality or erratic patterns of sleep. If you suspect this is the case, try to get into a regular pattern of rest by keeping the same approximate bedtime for a few weeks. By establishing a regular routine, your mind and body are likely to become programmed to sleep more easily.
- To induce restful sleep, take a soothing bedtime drink such as camomile tea, listen to a favourite piece of relaxing music, or vaporise a sleep-inducing essential oil such as lavender.
- If you know that when you wake up it takes a while to begin to feel human, make sure that you give yourself enough time to wake up before you begin your day, by getting up fifteen minutes or so earlier than absolutely necessary. By giving yourself this extra buffer of time you can avoid feeling stressed and pressured at a time when you are at less than your best. How you use this extra time is totally up to you: it could involve a specially long bath or shower, an extra long breakfast, or just a few minutes to sit down and gather your thoughts together.
- One of the best ways of waking up and revitalising yourself is to take a shower or bath using a bath or shower gel that includes refreshing and stimulating citrus essential oils. The combined action of the oils and the stimulating effect of the running water gives us one of the most pleasurable ways of kicking off the day.
- If you have sleep problems and wake feeling exhausted, avoid the temptation to rely on sleeping pills in order to get to sleep. Not only do these create potential addiction problems if used

constantly, but they also have the undesirable effect of making us feel drowsy during the day. Explore other options instead, such as valerian or passiflora tablets, or avena sativa compound. These should gently but effectively help you to achieve a relaxed night's sleep without the problems associated with conventional sleeping tablets.

- If you know that you don't feel your best on waking, always avoid going to sleep during the day, since this can make you feel the opposite of invigorated. It can also have the undesirable effect of making you feel rather depressed and disoriented. If you feel sleepiness coming on, try some of the invigorating measures listed above in order to keep going until the sleepiness has worn off. You are likely to feel much better for not letting the drowsiness take over.

Working in harmony with our energy potential

One of the most important things to bear in mind as we explore the concept of optimum energy levels is always to aim at achievable goals based on realistic expectations for ourselves.

In other words, if we have a history of poor mental and physical stamina, coupled with a persistent tendency to develop recurrent minor health problems, the chances are that we are going to have to rebuild our energy reserves slowly and steadily. We may also have to accept that our energy levels will always be lower than those who have a more dynamic energy potential. What counts, however, is that we should make the most of our individual energy potential rather than compare ourselves unrealistically and unfavourably with others.

On the other hand, do not be misled into thinking that this approach is a soft option which allows us to sink into accepting that a lack-lustre experience of health and vitality is our lot in life. Once we have a realistic idea of what we want, we can begin to make the changes that will release our individual potential for high-level health and well-being. The secret of success is always to compare your current progress with what you were capable of in the past, so that you create your own guidelines within which to assess your achievements.

The alternative medical approach to energy

If your answer to more than one of the following questions is negative, there is a strong chance that you could benefit from appropriate alternative medical treatment:

• Do you feel that you positively want to carry out certain tasks at home or at work?
• Do you find that you can sit and relax without falling asleep?
• Can you sit and concentrate on reading a document for more than a few minutes without your concentration wandering?
• Do you have less than one or two colds or other minor infections a year?
• Can you fall asleep easily and wake refreshed?
• Can you keep up the pace at work without chemical stimulants such as tea and coffee?
• Are you free of anxious or depressive thoughts most of the time?
• Do you positively enjoy your food, or do you eat mainly from habit, boredom, or in search of comfort?

Vital energy

At your initial assessment by an alternative medical practitioner such as a homoeopath, acupuncturist, Chinese or Western medical herbalist, you may be surprised at being asked what sort of energy levels you experience. This often seems an unusual question within the context of a medical interview, because conventional medicine pays little attention to this aspect of our experience of health unless, of course, energy levels may have a bearing on confirming or ruling out the suspected diagnosis of a medical condition.

Alternative therapists, on the other hand, are very concerned to establish the health of a patient's energy levels. This is because the presence or absence of abundant emotional, mental and physical energy levels are seen as a fundamental clue to the basic level of health experienced by the patient. Taking on board this alternative perspective can lead us to regard our health in a subtly different light, seeing good health as much more than a quality we experience in the absence of a diagnosable illness.

From an alternative medical perspective, the experience of genuinely good health means mind, emotions and body being in a fundamental state of harmony which involves freedom from the limitations of pain, exhaustion, and distress. However much this sounds a tall order, it is amazing how many patients who consult an alternative therapist in order to treat their asthma, eczema, irritable bowel syndrome, or migraines, find not only that the specific symptoms of their condition improve, but also that they experience improved energy levels, emotional well-being and physical resilience as a surprising by-product of their treatment.

This happens because an alternative therapist is not concerned with temporary or haphazard suppression of symptoms, but with a treatment that will stimulate the whole organism into a renewed state of balance. When this has been achieved, symptoms depart as the body's own curative mechanism kicks in. As a result, once symptoms have been effectively dealt with by the body's defence mechanism, they should remain absent unless the body later encounters excessive stress.

Stimulation of vital energy

Therapies such as homoeopathy, acupuncture, or reflexology are understood to work by stimulating the body's curative mechanisms through boosting energy levels. Homoeopathy regards an unseen energy field called the vital force as responsible for maintaining good health or throwing up symptoms of illness that alert us to the fact that the body needs help in order to get back on track. An appropriate homoeopathic remedy, which fits the patient's individual combination of symptoms as closely as possible, appears to act as a catalyst, giving the energy boost needed for the body's self-healing capacity to resolve the problem.

In acupuncture, the insertion of acupuncture needles at various points stimulates unseen energy channels called meridians in order to regulate energy flow. Reflexologists, on the other hand, work specifically with the feet, pressing identifiable points called reflexes which are believed to correspond to specific organs in the body. This pressure should boost the energy in the whole system, enabling the body to throw off symptoms of illness which may have become persistent.

Appropriate alternative treatment will not transform us overnight into dynamos of vitality. However, when it is used effectively, it can strengthen our individual constitutions to the point where we experience our potential for optimum energy production most of the time.

Basic techniques for strengthening energy levels

The following advice gives you the basic tools needed for a fundamental boost of energy levels. By acting on this advice, we should be able to make full use of our potential for maximum health and balanced energy release.

You will notice that this advice is designed to improve our experience of well-being on a range of emotional and physical levels, bearing out the basic premise that we only experience maximum energy when mind, emotions and body are in maximum harmony. As a result, you should find that these energy-stimulating techniques have long-term effects; they are intended to rectify fundamental and ingrained habits which compromise our potential for maximum energy production.

Identifying energy boosters and drainers

As we set to work improving our levels of vitality and well-being, it can be very helpful to identify the factors responsible for boosting and draining energy levels. By doing so, we can begin the process of establishing the overall balance of these factors in our everyday experience. Most important of all, once we have identified our vulnerable areas, we can initiate the positive changes needed to reach our energy goals.

Energy boosters
- High-quality eating
- Good-quality sleep
- Energising exercise
- Positive thinking
- Herbal tonics
- Breathing techniques
- Stimulating relationships

Energy drainers
- Junk foods
- Lack of, or poor quality, sleep
- Lack of exercise
- Long-term stress
- Absence of fun
- Addictive behaviour
- Destructive relationships

Energy-boosting measures

Eating for energy

If we want sustained energy levels, we must first consider the quality of the foods we eat regularly. Unfortunately, many of us are tricked into believing that having a sugary snack or fizzy drink is the best way to stimulate energy levels when we are flagging. This mistaken information is readily passed on to us through seductive advertising (an advertising campaign recently portrayed white sugar as a 'natural' energy source), while trendy carbonated drinks are usually associated with images of youth, vitality and sporting activities.

While it is true that refined (white table) sugar and its products will give a temporary rush of energy, this is only short-lived. As a result, when we come down from this energy rush we shall probably feel no further forward and often crave another sugar boost in order to keep up the pace. Once we give in to this, our blood sugar levels peak again, only to be followed by another slump in mental and physical energy.

If this pattern of eating continues long enough, it can cause very erratic blood sugar levels which constantly peak and trough through the day. This not only leaves us open to erratic mental and physical performance, it can also lead to potential health problems such as weight gain, dental cavities and low blood sugar (hypoglycaemia) or high blood sugar (hyperglycaemia) levels. The last two problems can cause very similar unpleasant symptoms, including irritability, jitteriness, lack of concentration, headaches, palpitations (consciousness of a rapid or irregular heartbeat), digestive disorders and sleep problems.

The reason for the problems associated with a diet high in refined white sugar is simple: once our blood sugar level is raised by eating or drinking something sweet, our bodies respond by stimulating the pancreas to secrete insulin in order to bring our blood sugar levels back to a cruising level. If we regularly take too much sugar, because we constantly feel tired and in need of a quick burst of energy, we can end up with a trigger-happy pancreas that is constantly under pressure to keep blood sugar levels under control.

It is also worth bearing in mind that blood sugar levels are even more disrupted if a sugary snack is combined with caffeine, which also has a reputation for destabilising blood sugar. Imagine the impact on the body if we regularly snack on chocolate (which contains sugar and caffeine), washed down with a sugary, fizzy drink which contains a high proportion of sugar and often caffeine), plus coffee to follow. If this continues long enough, the pancreas becomes exhausted and unable to carry out its task efficiently.

To avoid riding this energy roller-coaster, we need to distinguish between foods that give us sustained energy release, and quick-fix foods that lead to more problems than they are worth. Refined carbohydrates fall in to the latter category and should be kept to an absolute minimum in the diet, or eliminated altogether if possible. They include biscuits, cakes, sweets, fizzy drinks, chocolate and sweetened convenience foods. It can be a sobering experience to check the list of ingredients on any prepared food and discover how frequently sugar appears.

When checking labels, remember that refined sugar can appear in a range of disguises that include glucose, corn syrup, maltose and dextrose. Don't forget to check savoury food labels as well, because refined sugar can pop up in the most unexpected places such as cans of baked beans.

The foods that promote optimum energy release are also classed as carbohydrates, but in their complex or unrefined form. They should be included regularly in our daily eating plans if we want to achieve balanced energy levels. They include whole grain products (such as bread made from wholemeal flour), lentils, beans, potatoes and vegetables. Foods in the complex carbohydrate group take longer to digest than refined carbohydrates and, as a result, release their sugar content more slowly. This gives us a slow-release effect which leads to greater stamina and energy levels which are sustained and less inclined to peak and trough.

Fruit is also an important source of energy, containing a form of sugar called fructose. Although this is more readily broken down than the complex carbohydrates listed above, fruit will still cause less instability in blood sugar levels than refined sugar (sucrose). So snacking occasionally on a piece of fruit when energy levels are lagging will result in a helpful boost of energy that is less likely to be followed by exhaustion than it would be if we had a chocolate or sweet. In practical terms, if we have a busy schedule it is obviously much more convenient to munch on an apple or a banana when we snatch a quick break than to tuck into a plate of wholemeal past and lentils.

When moving to an eating pattern that gives us the best chanc of sustained energy release, don't be misled into thinking you hav to change everything at once. Not only is this very daunting (encour aging us to put it off that little bit longer until the right time come around), it can also result in a terrific shock to the system. For th best results, begin steadily to substitute complex carbohydrates fo refined products. In other words, as your white flour and pasta ar used up, replace them with wholemeal varieties. It is the same witl breakfast cereals: substitute whole grain muesli with dried fruit fo refined breakfast cereals which include a high amount of refine sugar and salt.

When buying snacks, avoid chocolate bars and doughnut (which are astronomically high in refined sugar and fat) and op instead for mixes of sunflower seeds (which are especially good a stabilising blood sugar levels while keeping cravings at bay), bite size pieces of fresh fruit and unsalted nuts, or dried fruit bar (checking that they do not include chemical preservatives). If thi sounds too fussy, just take a couple of washed apples or pears an a banana to work.

At home, slowly change your pattern of eating by having a coupl of nights where you choose to eat brown rice, beans or pulses rathe than red meat, quiches and pastries. This need not involve a hug effort, because you can now buy ready-cooked brown rice, beans an lentils. Although this is undeniably a more expensive way to enjo these ingredients, if you have a very busy life they enable you t enjoy their nutritional and energy-giving qualities without waitin, for them to cook for hours at the end of a busy day.

If you are addicted to coffee, avoid going 'cold turkey' because th withdrawal symptoms can put you off giving up for good. Instead slowly and steadily replace an increasing number of cups of coffe each day with one of the coffee-substitutes available. These are grain or fig-based powders, often flavoured with chicory, and are mucl more palatable than the dandelion coffee that was the only coffe substitute on offer in the sixties and seventies.

Other possibilities include fruit-flavoured teas, or the occasional cup of herbal tisane. However, do experiment with a number of possibilities, rather than try one herbal tea and dismiss it as not for you. The potential flavours are extremely varied, and it can take a little while before you hit on an appealing taste. Also look out for combinations of fruit flavours such as apple and cinnamon, or mixtures of citrus and berries which appeal to those of us who like a sharp, invigorating taste.

Herbal tonics

A herbal tonic can also be included in the diet in the form of root ginger tea. Although commonly used as a spice in cooking, ginger also has a powerful reputation for its stimulating, tonic properties. Apart from providing a general tonic for the circulatory system, ginger also, it is claimed, has antioxidant and anti-inflammatory properties. If you occasionally crave something sweet, you may find a small amount of crystallised ginger satisfying. Certainly, it has such a pungent taste that it is unlikely to be eaten in large quantities. Alternatively, a cup of ginger root tea can be a pleasant way of clearing the mind and stimulating the taste buds. For directions on how to make it, see p. 183.

Ginseng can also be taken as a supplement if you feel in need of a general boost to your system. Although rather extravagant claims have been made for ginseng as a virtual cure-all for any problem, there appears to be enough evidence to suggest that it may be beneficial as a general tonic.

Dr Andrew Weil's research shows that this supplement abounds in biologically active substances that influence the pituitary–adrenal axis. As a result of this hormonal influence, some of the potential positive effects include greater energy production, increased libido, improved skin texture, and generally enhanced natural resistance in the system as a whole.

In using ginseng as a general tonic, it is important to take it daily for two months in order to give it a fair trial, since it can take this long before positive effects become apparent. However, caution should be used in situations where high blood pressure or insomnia are a problem, because ginseng may aggravate these conditions.

Energising sleep

Sound, good-quality sleep is absolutely essential if we are aiming for optimum levels of energy and vitality. When we sleep we give our vital organs a chance to rest, our immune systems a chance to recharge and renew themselves and our subconscious the chance to release emotions in the safe form of dreams.

As a result, if we are deprived of good-quality sleep for an extended period we shall probably begin to feel permanently tired, irritable, anxious, and generally washed-out. Additional physical problems may also begin to appear, such as an irritating tendency to develop recurrent colds or other minor illnesses, due to a reduced production of the white blood cells that fight infection.

If we are aiming for the best-quality rest, it is very important to understand at the outset that everyone has individual requirements when it comes to the actual number of hours of sleep needed each night. In other words, there is little point in struggling to have eight hours' rest each night if we actually only need six hours of deep sleep in order to feel completely refreshed.

This is especially important, because it has been suggested that too much sleep can, paradoxically, lead to some of the same problems as too little rest. These can include poor concentration, reduced ability to make correct decisions and mood swings. On the other hand, if you know from experience that when you have ten hours' sleep a night you fire on all four cylinders, but if you are deprived of this amount you feel as though you have been dragged through a hedge backwards, clearly your constitutional make-up demands more sleep than the average.

Once you have worked out the optimum amount of sleep you need each night in order to wake feeling fully refreshed, it makes sense to try to stick to this as your general rule. Of course this doesn't mean that you have to become a hermit and turn your back on a lively social life (this would hardly indicate a change in lifestyle which promotes balanced good health); but you should try to get your optimum quota of sound sleep on the majority of nights.

If you have a couple of late nights, don't think that you have to have hours of extra sleep in order to catch up. The reality is much simpler: all you have to do is return to your normal routine of sleep as quickly as possible and your system should then settle easily enough into its familiar pattern.

On the other hand, in certain circumstances we can find that our sleep pattern seems to go completely off the rails. These can include any severe shock or grief, extreme personal or professional stress (including financial problems), travelling on long-distance flights, hormonal changes linked to pre-menstrual syndrome, or menopausal symptoms including night sweats which can severely disrupt sleep. See the section on insomnia on p. 160 for practical suggestions for improving short-term sleep problems.

Above all, remember that panicking is one of the very worst things we can do if sleep problems descend. Ironically, once we become anxious about not sleeping at night, we substantially reduce our chances of falling asleep. Although it may be very difficult to resist getting uptight, try instead to listen to some soothing music, read a favourite book, listen to the radio, or make a cup of camomile tea.

Sedative and stimulating foods

It can be very helpful, if surprising, to realise that certain foods have a strong soothing or wakefulness-inducing effect on our systems. It therefore makes sense to include the more stimulating items in the earlier part of the day in order to boost our vitality when we most need it, and deliberately use sedative foods before we sleep.

Stimulating, energising foods include whole grain cereals, fruit, complex carbohydrates such as potatoes and easily-digested forms of protein such as fish and chicken, or pulses and cereals combined together in one meal. Small amounts of protein eaten during the day can stimulate the secretion of dopamine; this in turn is converted into adrenalin, which is also produced when we are under stress, to give us the kick needed for action.

Unsalted, unroasted nuts and seeds can also be included as snacks during the day in order to keep energy levels topped up and contribute to a general state of being alert and clear-headed. This is due to their natural content of selenium and boron, trace minerals which apparently contribute to mental alertness and clarity of thought.

Foods that have the opposite effect include bananas, which contain the relaxing and naturally anti-depressant amino acid tryptophan. Other sedative foods include avocado, peanut butter, dairy foods, lettuce and oranges (which contain a relaxant called bromine). These are ideal for a light late-night snack to help us avoid those hunger pangs which can interfere with a sound night's sleep.

On the other hand, you should consciously avoid certain habits which can contribute to a poor night's rest. These include heavy meals late at night and large quantities of alcohol. Apart from the general health hazards associated with excessive drinking, it is worth bearing in mind that large amounts of alcohol can also act as a stimulant. On the other hand, a small measure of spirits, or a glass of wine taken with food early in the evening, can have the opposite, relaxing effect. This is partly because, when alcohol is taken with food, it is released more slowly into the bloodstream.

Energising exercise

In any discussion about boosting and balancing energy levels, we shall inevitably need to explore the important role played by exercise. Unfortunately, this is the moment when many of us may mentally switch off, thinking that running half marathons, slavishly using a stair master, or sweatily gasping through a step class is just not for us. If this is your first reaction, think again and stay with this section of the chapter, since we shall be discussing a very different form of exercise and motivation.

For the sort of movement we are going to explore, you do not need the latest, most expensive and fashionable fitness clothes. And perhaps most important of all, you do not need to have a model-like figure with cellulite-free thighs, or bankrupt yourself by joining a wickedly expensive gym.

In my experience (both personal and as a practitioner listening to the varied accounts of my patients), it often seems that many of us take out a hefty subscription to a gym because we feel under pressure to take some radical action and get fit. It is no coincidence that this most commonly happens in the first weeks of January. Sadly, many of us don't take our commitments into account when we do this and find that after an initial flurry of exercise activity, we give up because it is difficult to sustain our good intentions. This often has the undesirable effect of making us feel guilty as well as physically unfit.

The reason why we fall into this trap is quite simple: we tend to be too radical and ambitious in what we want to achieve when we set out on the road to physical fitness. Ironically, this is especially the case with those who have a sedentary and inactive lifestyle. Because they want to achieve too much too soon (thinking that radical problems demand radical solutions), the chances are that they will not sustain the amount of effort required.

The quick-fix problem

The way we feel about exercise often reflects our basic need for the fast solution. The marketing of everything from painkillers to computers stresses the importance of meeting the needs of individuals who have no time to waste being distracted by pain or an inefficient computer system. As a result of this high-pressure hard sell, many of us feel that we have to approach physical fitness in the same way, by going out for a physical assault in order to sculpt our bodies into shape in double-quick time.

The most effective energy-balancing forms of exercise (such as yoga and T'ai chi) encourage us to work gradually and in harmony with our bodies, effectively reducing the risk of injury and trauma. Both these systems provide us with a form of meditation and relaxation in movement, so that at the end of a class we should feel more balanced, relaxed and energised than we did when we began.

However, it is important not to be misled into thinking that this is a rather soft option that requires little effort and so results in little physical conditioning. In fact, quite the opposite is true, because yoga in particular can liberate our bodies into a state of more muscular strength and suppleness than we could ever have imagined, especially with the more demanding systems such as power yoga.

Both T'ai chi and yoga appear to stimulate vital energy levels (called chi in the former and prana in the latter) through the use of specific breathing techniques during controlled physical movement. These forms of exercise are thus completely compatible with those forms of alternative medicine which stimulate vital energy such as acupuncture and homoeopathy.

If you want to start improving your energy potential, the best place to start is by enrolling in a T'ai chi or yoga class once a week. This is an easily achievable commitment, and you can ensure steady progress by making attendance at this class a priority you refuse to skip. Once you have been to half a dozen or so sessions, you should have learned enough of the basic techniques to continue practising at home. At this stage you may find that using one of the increasingly large range of video tapes will help to guide you through your practice away from class. On the other hand, don't be tempted to skip the lessons and start this way, because it really is very important to learn how to do the postures and movements correctly at the outset with the guidance of a good teacher. Bear in mind that the postures will only benefit you if they are done well, otherwise you may inadvertently do more harm than good.

For more general advice on how to achieve a balanced fitness regime based on your individual needs, consult Chapter Four ('Exercise Boosters'). This gives more detailed and directive advice on integrating regular physical movement into your lifestyle.

Positive thinking

If we regularly feel exhausted and drained, it is worth considering how much our state of mind is affecting our outlook on life and our reactions to others. It is amazing how we can very easily slip into thinking in a negative way without even realising it; unfortunately this can become a self-fulfilling dynamic.

Once we begin to think along these lines, we may be astonished at how unwanted emotions such as anxiety, anger, or resentment drain us of positive mental, emotional and physical power and energy.

These negative emotions can distort our view of the world around us, leading us unconsciously to react to events in a way more likely to generate a negative, rather than a positive, outcome. Sadly, this sort of experience reinforces our pessimistic viewpoint, making us even more downbeat about our expectations.

If, over time, this becomes an ingrained part of our approach to life, it can drain us of a significant amount of vitality. The resulting negative energy spiral goes something like this: We feel generally low so we can't be bothered to eat in a balanced way; as a result, we feel so tired that the very thought of any physical exercise is out of the question; so we begin to feel guilty as well as generally lacking self-esteem. This can make us turn to comfort eating as a refuge, which can lead to weight gain, which makes us feel even worse about ourselves. We may find by this stage that we feel less confident at work and that our personal relationships are suffering as a result of our negative perception of ourselves.

Thank goodness, however, that a positive spiral is also possible, which turns this negative picture on its head. Positive changes usually start by taking a very small but significant step to improve the situation. This could be embarking on alternative medical treatment which gives us a perceptible energy boost. We are then encouraged to look at the quality of our diet and make changes that support a further experience of good health. By this stage we are probably steadily gaining in energy levels, with the result that we are in a more positive frame of mind for taking on a realistic amount of exercise. This raises our levels of vitality a notch or two further, and increases the likelihood of boosted self-confidence and self-esteem. If we have problems that need sorting out, we are likely to feel sufficiently positive and in command to initiate changes in our professional or personal lives that we may have been putting off for ages. By this stage, our lives may not be perfect, but we are well on the road to living life from a positive rather than a negative perspective. Remember that this is not a static process, but an evolving state which grows and changes with us as we gain in confidence and self-knowledge.

Self-perception and self-esteem

The way we present ourselves or approach others can also significantly influence a positive or negative outcome. In others words, if we give an impression of being hesitant, pessimistic, or lacking in enthusiasm when we try to influence positively someone in a position of seniority, there is a fighting chance that we shall be unsuccessful. On the other hand, if we approach each situation as a challenge, applying a confident, energetic and positive approach to the problem, we are actively supporting the possibility of a successful outcome. Even if we do not achieve our goal, we are less likely to be psychologically demolished if we continue to adopt a realistically positive perspective. By doing so we are empowered to use the experience as a way of expanding our knowledge of ourselves, rather than as an opportunity for metaphorically beating ourselves about the head for being so useless.

Although this may sound a tall order for those of us who are bogged down by constantly adopting a downbeat perspective on life, you may be surprised to learn that even well-established thought patterns of this kind can be influenced by appropriate psychological support. Systems such as cognitive therapy can teach us to identify the negative thought processes and patterns we unwittingly use when confronted with certain events.

Once we have established where our vulnerable areas lie, we are in a position to adapt our reactions to challenging situations. As a result, we are likely to find that, by adopting a more balanced perspective, problems which previously seemed insurmountable are turned into manageable situations with a positive outcome. This frees up an astonishing amount of energy that would previously have been worthlessly squandered in worrying about problems without finding a solution.

For more information on avoiding the pitfalls of self-sabotage through adopting positive thought patterns, see Chapter Five ('Mental and Emotional Boosters').

Energising emotions

It may initially sound a little odd to speak of our emotions having a negative or positive impact on our energy levels, but if we adopt a consistently holistic view of our health (rather than a cosmetic or partial holistic approach) we need to consider our emotional environment and its overall impact on our levels of health and vitality.

You may be very good at paying attention to the quality of your food and the amount of rest and relaxation you get, but forget to consider how much emotional balance you have in your close relationships. In other words, you need to think about whether you spend enough time in the company of positive people who make you feel stimulated, supported and energised, or whether your time is dominated by draining personalities or circumstances which sap your optimism and vitality.

The latter can be easily identified as the sort of people who, when you eagerly share your excitement and enthusiasm with them, automatically respond with a cautionary 'But what if . . . ?'. Although many of us can cope with this as an occasional response without major dents being made in our resolve and commitment, too frequent exposure to a dampening of our enthusiasm will probably lead eventually to less energy for the tasks in hand. A single drop of water will not eat away a stone, but if the same stone is exposed long enough to the persistent dripping of water it will eventually become eroded. However, many of us have probably enjoyed the opposite experience of spending time in upbeat and stimulating company, which galvanises us into positive action where we may have been slightly wavering before.

Although it would be foolish to demand an impossibly positive life where negative influences were non-existent, we need to be on our guard against having to deal with too many energy-draining experiences on a day-to-day basis. As in all other aspects of our life, what we are striving for is an optimum sense of balance in our emotional life so that we have enough positive energy to keep us on track.

Protecting the positive

Before we can take action to boost the amount of positive input in our lives, we first have to evaluate honestly and realistically the general quality of relationships in our lives. Consider the wide range of social contacts you enjoy, including friends, your partner, family members, colleagues and anyone you talk to on a short but regular basis (such as shopkeepers or neighbours). How do you feel after spending time with most of these? Optimistic and cheered, rather negative and down in the dumps, or just fairly neutral and balanced?

If you feel pretty good about these relationships as a whole, the chances are that you have achieved a general balance where most of your communication with others is positive or neutral. On the other hand, if you feel that you tend to gravitate towards those who confide in you about their problems and leave you feeling washed-out, you need to take action or run a serious risk of emotional 'burn out'.

You may need to be fairly ruthless in limiting exposure to relationships which have the effect of putting you down, or eroding your sense of self-esteem. Unfortunately, a negative perspective is contagious: too much contact with people who keep planting ideas in our heads about our inadequacies or shortcomings, and we can develop an unrealistically negative state of mind. Instead, make sure that you spend as much time as possible with those who value your company, make you laugh, listen carefully to what you have to say and generally bolster your sense of self-esteem.

Above all, don't fall into the trap of hanging on to people who have a negative effect on you because they make you feel needed. Unwittingly, many of us fall foul of this situation with people who are emotionally very needy but do not move on after we have given them all the support we can. If this happens, we may well not be able to detach ourselves from a difficult situation without feeling a huge amount of guilt. If this continues for too long, we will be faced with a stark choice between continuing in a relationship which has a draining effect on us, or deciding to draw the relationship to a close.

First steps in assertiveness

If we feel we must end a difficult relationship or put it 'on hold' for a while, it is extremely important to be as calm and assertive as possible. This may be difficult for us if our self-esteem has become very fragile, but it is not impossible, once we know the general guidelines for getting our point across with the maximum amount of impact.

The first rule in adopting an assertive stance is to speak your mind in a calm, clear and constructive way. Always remember that being assertive is quite different to being angry, because assertiveness involves remaining in command of a situation. Once you lose your temper, you can no longer see a situation in a balanced light and are likely to over-react at the slightest provocation. Being on a permanently 'short fuse' is also exhausting, because we can expend an alarming amount of energy in an outburst of anger.

Bear in mind that asserting yourself in a potential situation of conflict is likely in the end to lead to greater mutual understanding. However, once you descend into an inflammatory argument, it is likely in the long run to lead to more conflict and reduced understanding.

If you are bringing an unsatisfactory relationship to a halt, it is best to work out what you want to say in advance so that you express yourself as clearly as possible. This also gives you a chance to prepare yourself for a range of possible responses. At the outset, try to negotiate a situation where the person you are communicating with feels that you are taking their concerns into account rather than dismissing them without a thought. If you can also make them feel that they will benefit in some way from your decision, there is a greater chance that your exchange will have an ultimately positive outcome.

Three steps can help us frame what we need to say when we are approaching a difficult situation. These include:

- Describing the problematic situation as succinctly, objectively and correctly as possible.
- Conveying your own feelings about the situation as clearly as possible, avoid as far as you can making the other party feel guilty

or giving the impression that you are being unduly judgemental.
• Proposing a change in the general situation, or a realistic way in which the other party could change their behaviour in order to give everybody more breathing space.

If the person you are speaking to constantly tries to evade or change the subject, make a point of not losing your temper, but coming back calmly and repeatedly to the point that you need to make. Make sure that the situation is resolved in a way that leaves you feeling that you have conveyed what you needed to say; there is then a good chance that you will not be haunted by guilt or suppressed emotions. Most important of all, once you have taken action to move on from relationships which drain you, you will rapidly find that you have more energy at your disposal than you imagined.

Emotional enemies of energy
It is astonishing how much of our basic supply of energy and vitality is drained away when we suffer from anxiety and fear on a regular or protracted basis. Although short-term emotional stress can give us the 'edge' that we need to perform well (such as the jittery and hyped-up feelings we may experience before giving a presentation or meeting a short-term deadline), long-term free-floating anxiety can sap us of our basic 'get up and go'. Basic feelings of fear that are not associated with any obvious trigger can also have the unpleasant effect of inhibiting us from initiating any positive action we might take to improve our lives, since changes are usually interpreted by someone in a highly anxious state as threats rather than an opportunity for a change for the better.

Chronic anxiety and fear also tend to have an adverse impact on our sleep and eating patterns, which will also contribute to performing below our optimum levels on emotional, mental and physical levels. This, in turn, can further damage our sense of self-confidence, leading to the sort of downward energy spiral described in the 'Positive thinking' section above. We can, however, take positive steps to contain anxiety and fear by following the advice in Chapter Five ('Mental and Emotional Boosters').

Breathing techniques

The suggestion that we breathe incompletely or incorrectly comes as a shock to many people. After all, we do it without thinking every day and stay alive as a result. However, many of us are using very little of our potential lung capacity when we breathe in and out. As a result of faulty breathing techniques we often compromise our capacity for relaxation, clear-headedness and vitality.

It is quite astonishing that something as basic as the way we breathe can have a profound effect on making us feel full of energy or extremely calm and relaxed. However, in order to make maximum use of this invaluable potential, we must learn subtle ways of controlling how we breathe. Once we have learnt to do this, we have an astonishingly powerful tool at our disposal which can balance our energy levels quickly and effectively.

The basic importance of posture

There is little point in discussing how to breathe in a deep and balanced way, without first considering how we hold ourselves when we sit or stand. Many of us tend to hunch our upper spine and shoulders when we walk or sit at a desk. If this habit continues long enough, it leads to a permanent slouch which can have a profound effect on how we look and feel. A hunched-over spine leads to backaches and pains and may increase our susceptibility to painful conditions such as sciatica or a slipped disc. Apart from the physical problems, it also plays a profoundly important negative role in draining us of energy and confidence.

Try this simple exercise next time you are feeling tired or stressed and you may be surprised at what you discover. There is a major likelihood that your shoulders are tense and hunched up towards your ears, your jaw clenched tightly and your whole arm tense, with the hand often clenched into a fist or gripping something uncomfortably tightly, such as a pen. If you are walking, there is also a strong chance that your head is held forwards and downwards, so that you are more inclined to look at the ground than at what is happening at eye level or above. This often has the unconscious effect of reinforcing feelings of negativity, outwardly reflecting the way you feel inside, and it may also influence the way others unconsciously pick up these clues and respond to us, with the result that the vicious circle continues and gets stronger.

If we also notice the way we are breathing in the situation outlined above, we shall probably find that we are breathing in a rapid, irregular and shallow way, using only a small portion of our upper chest. This common habit has the unwanted but powerful effect of promoting feelings of tension, anxiety, fatigue and despondency.

The reason for this is straightforward: when we breathe in a quick, shallow way we adversely affect the ratio of oxygen (taken in when we inhale) and carbon dioxide (breathed out as we exhale). When these two gases exist in an unbalanced relationship to each other in our bodies, we begin to experience a range of feelings that can extend from mild instability of mood to outright panic. Because we are only using a small amount of our lung capacity to breathe, we may also feel that we are lacking in concentration and physical energy because not enough oxygen is reaching our circulatory systems. In addition, waste products are not being eliminated sufficiently thoroughly, due to the incomplete exhalation of carbon dioxide.

Pointers to balanced posture

Optimum postural alignment does not consist in having a spine that is held rigidly in place as straight as a poker, any more than it involves slumping and slouching in the way described above. It is essential to appreciate at the outset that our own instinctive sense will tell us when we have achieved the most balanced postural position for ourselves.

This can be helped enormously by taking lessons in the Alexander Technique. In an Alexander session a teacher will concentrate on developing with an individual pupil a finely-tuned awareness of balanced posture when doing simple tasks such as sitting down, or rising from a chair.

Learning about the Alexander Technique involves discovering a great deal about how we use our bodies in stressful situations to armour or protect ourselves against perceived problems. These need not be physical threats, but are often linked to difficulties such as an over-demanding workload, an unreasonable boss, disagreements with a partner, or an unexpected bill that appears at just the wrong time.

When we learn how we react to these sorts of problems, by identifying and locating the tensed muscle groups, we can take the first steps towards freeing ourselves up physically so that we have the choice of reacting in a different way. As a result, we can also enjoy the increased energy which comes from releasing tense muscles which can become almost rock hard in defensive positions. For more general information on postural awareness, see the section on the Alexander Technique on p. 122 of Chapter Four.

We can take the first simple steps to achieving optimum postural alignment by experimenting with the following advice in order to find out what suits us best as individuals.

- When sitting, walking or standing, make sure that your head is balanced lightly on your neck, with your shoulders relaxed and a good distance from your ears. If you feel that your shoulders are tense and hunched up towards your head, consciously let them relax downwards as you breathe out fully.

- Pay attention to your jaw, in order to discover how much tension is held there without your normally being aware of it. If you find that your upper and lower jaws are held in a tightly-clenched position, consciously relax both the muscles surrounding the hinge joint of your jaw and the muscles of your face. While you are doing this, check that you also release and soften the muscles at the sides of your neck and shoulders. If you do this correctly, you should find that your shoulders drop an inch or so as they are relaxed.

- Become aware of the amount of tension held in your whole arm, from the muscles at the top of the shoulder to the tips of your fingers. We can quickly assess how unrelaxed our arm muscles are by noticing how tightly we grip an object such as a pen or a doorknob. The chances are that we put in far too much effort when we carry out simple tasks such as writing, by gripping the pen far more tightly than necessary.

In fact, if we over-tense our finger and hand muscles in this way, we are actually making it harder for ourselves to write in a relaxed way, in addition to using up energy that could be put more productively into other tasks. If you discover that you are clenching your hands tightly, you will find that this spreads all the way up the arm muscles into the shoulder, neck and jaw. This in turn can have a domino effect, tensing up the sheet of large muscles that covers our backs and spine.

We can begin to remedy the situation by consciously softening and relaxing the muscles in our hands, so that when we grip anything we do it consciously, lightly and with the minimum amount of force needed to accomplish whatever it is we want to do. One simple way of guarding against this tension happening automatically is to avoid doing things without thinking; we put too much effort into something because we are operating on automatic pilot. Once we have every task under our conscious control, we can choose to do it with an appropriate, rather than excessive, amount of effort.

- Once you have become aware of areas of tension in your upper body, bring your attention to the whole of your back, trying consciously to let go of any parts that feel tight or stiff. Any areas that are stubbornly unrelaxed might benefit from a regular back and shoulder massage. More well-established back problems may require treatment from an osteopath or chiropractor. An occasional complete body massage can be extremely helpful in helping to relax the muscles in the whole body, including those that are often neglected such as the legs and the feet.

- Once you have generally relaxed your muscles as much as possible, you can concentrate on achieving a balanced and comfortable posture before you begin your breathing techniques. You will experience maximum alignment and balance if you imagine that you have a string pulling you gently upwards from the top of your head. Your shoulders should be relaxed and away from your ears, while your chest should feel lifted upwards and outwards. When standing, tuck in the base of the spine, making sure that the bottom doesn't stick out too far, while tightening the muscles of the abdomen. Relax the thighs, knees and calf muscles as much as possible, making sure that your weight is equally and firmly balanced between both feet.

If you have achieved balanced posture, you should find that you are not putting undue weight on the balls of the feet or the heels; your weight should be equally distributed over the complete surface of each sole of the foot. When sitting or kneeling, try to keep the spine comfortably straight and the weight equally distributed on both sides.

Energising breathing techniques

When we are breathing consciously and correctly we should inhale and exhale fully, evenly and rhythmically. When we breathe in, we should feel our abdomens relaxing outwards as our lungs fill with air to their maximum capacity. When we breathe out, our abdomens should naturally flatten and contract inwards as air is expelled from the base of the lungs to the top. By using our lungs to their fullest capacity in this way, we increase the amount of oxygen that reaches the bloodstream. This gives our cells the maximum chance for cellular rejuvenation and revitalisation, increasing our energy levels and vitality.

Apart from the importance of breathing from the abdomen as mentioned above, there are specific breathing exercises used in the practice of yoga to clear the mind and energise the body. The two breathing techniques described below are thought to encourage increased flow of energy through the whole body. The first exercise should be done daily (ideally in the morning) as an energising way of starting the day. The second breathing technique may be used as a more short-term measure to clear the mind and give a quick energy boost.

Breathing exercise 1

Stand in the good posture outlined above. Clasp your hands under your chin, with your chin tilted gently downwards. Breathe in from the abdomen for a count of five, while lifting your elbows as high as they will comfortably go without straining. Breathe out for a count of five while exhaling through your mouth and tilting your head backwards. At the end of the exhale bring your elbows gently back together again and lower your head to its starting position. Repeat this exercise ten times in all. If you feel dizzy or light-headed when doing this for the first time, don't panic; just stop, breathe normally and start again when you feel ready. Remember never to force the breath and to take things at a pace that is comfortable for you. In time and with practice, it will become quite effortless.

Breathing exercise 2

Sit on your heels, keeping your spine as straight as possible and your head well balanced, with your eyes gazing straight ahead. Breathe in and out fully so that your abdomen expands and contracts gently. Blow out sharply while pulling in strongly with your abdominal muscles for ten blows. If you feel dizzy or light-headed, stop the exercise and breathe normally. Once you are familiar with this exercise you can build up to a set of sixty blows at a time. (NB: This exercise should be avoided by anyone who has a health problem such as high blood pressure or heart disease. If you are in any doubt about the suitability of this exercise for you, it is best to seek your GP's guidance and opinion.)

2

Immune System Boosters

Our immune systems are our basic defence against the constant invasions and attacks made on our bodies by micro-organisms in the environment. If our defences are working at the level of optimum efficiency, this secret war goes on without our knowledge, since we are unlikely to experience any noticeable symptoms of illness. On the other hand, if we feel as if we are constantly lurching from one infection to another; or are permanently under par, fatigued and plagued with minor symptoms that just won't go away, this would suggest that our immune systems are simply not getting to grips with the job in hand. The result need not be major illness, but the negative effect on the quality of our lives can be marked, since we are unlikely to feel as though we are 'firing on all four cylinders' when we are at work or play.

Since we are so dependent on our immune systems to protect us against a whole host of hostile invaders, learning how to support and protect these defences is the most fundamental first step we can take to maximising our potential for high-level health and vitality.

Once we learn the basic ways in which we can work in harmony with our body's own defences, we become far less dependent on medication to fight our battles for us. Too many of us feel uneasy about relying on frequent courses of antibiotics to keep recurrent infections at bay, not only because of undesirable side-effects, but also because this reliance on medication can leave too many of us feeling disempowered and lacking the necessary confidence in our body's own defences.

Understanding our immune systems

Before we explore ways of supporting our immune systems, we need a quick tour of the basic processes involved in order to grasp just how these defences work. Once we understand the basic mechanisms at work, we shall be in a much stronger position to know why certain factors support, and others depress our body's in-built defences.

The first line of defence

Our very first line of defence against intruding organisms is the most visible barrier: the skin. Most of us are primarily concerned with the cosmetic appearance of our skin, without considering the vitally important protective role it plays in maintaining our levels of optimum health. This essential covering is designed to keep things in (such as blood, vital organs and muscles) and hold our bodies in shape. But it also keeps unwelcome visitors out.

This is why any break in the skin can lead to infection, because abrasions and cuts destroy the skin's vitally important seal against outside invaders. Given this important function, the skin clearly needs to be protected and kept as supple and resilient as possible, to provide the best chance of keeping infection at bay.

The immune system links with every part of the body. It has the vital job of neutralising or destroying any invading micro-organisms so that we remain immune to infection. It is made up of a complex network of organs including the thymus gland, spleen, bone marrow, tonsils and lymphatic system. We are dependent upon special white cells called lymphocytes formed in the bone marrow and thymus gland, and blood protein molecules called antibodies for the immune system to do its job efficiently.

The nature of immunity

There are two different types of immunity. The first, called *passive* immunity, we are born with, or acquire through antibodies in our mother's milk if we have been breast-fed. This is an essential protection for small babies while they are developing the second type of immunity, referred to as *acquired* immunity. The latter develops in response to contact with any new bacteria or viruses. Once immunity has developed in response to these micro-organisms, it remains in the 'memory' of the immune system so that if we encounter the same micro-organism in the future, an aggressive response can be put into action very rapidly.

This ability to recognise and eliminate foreign invaders is one of the immune system's most impressive attributes, since it allows for the switching-on of a series of defence measures in double-quick time. The immune system is also astonishingly adept at diversifying its approach, so that it can mount an aggressive attack against a bewildering variety of potential invading organisms. However, contact with each micro-organism requires an individualised response. So, for example, we may acquire an immunity towards chicken pox, but we will need to develop a fresh immune response to the measles virus if we come in contact with it.

The immune system in action

When the immune system swings into action against an invader, the thymus gland produces T-cells which act together with B-cells (produced by the bone marrow). The B-lymphocytes produce antibodies to eliminate threatening organisms at the prompting of 'helper T-cells'. They also stop producing antibodies when told to by

41

'suppressor T-cells'. In addition, there are 'killer T-cells', designed to attack and destroy tumours and viruses. These cells are collectively called lymphocytes, and when they are working efficiently they produce effective antibodies against an invading organism. A swift response can be mounted against organisms recognised from the past, but antibody production may take a few days if the invading micro-organism is new. This is the time when swollen, painful glands appear, caused by white blood cells incubating a supply of antibodies in the lymph nodes. The main lymph nodes are located in the armpits, groin, and neck.

We also produce another type of white blood cell called phago-cytes in response to injury or infection. These are scavenger cells which devour microbes and debris.

How it can go wrong

It is essential that the immune system works in an efficient, balanced way if our bodies are to remain in good health. We shall be exploring ways of positively supporting the working of our defences later, but it is worth considering first some of the things that can go wrong with the delicate balance of the immune system.

• If the immune system becomes hypersensitive, it can start over-reacting to potentially harmless agents such as pollen, house dust, fungal spores, animal fur, and certain foods such as peanuts, fish, or shellfish. When this happens we experience an allergic reaction which can cause asthma, hay fever, food allergies, or eczema.

• In good health, our helper and suppressor T-cells are in a state of optimum balance, with the result that antibodies are in adequate supply when they are needed. However, if we develop a dominance of suppressor cells, our immune system becomes weakened or deficient. This can happen as a result of an inherited condition or an opportunistic viral infection such as HIV.

• It is possible for helper T-cells to do their job too enthusiastically, causing the immune system to attack body tissues because it can no longer differentiate between a threatening invader and harmless cells. Problems that occur as a result of this process are called auto-immune diseases and include rheumatoid arthritis, corneal ulcers and multiple sclerosis.

- Another, less obvious, category of less-than-perfect immune system functioning results in our just not getting to grips with one minor infection after another. This need not be a sinister or dramatic situation, but it can compromise our basic levels of health, well-being and zest for life. If this happens, we need to take stock and make changes in our lifestyle to support the effective working of our body's own defences.

Immune system stress factors

The following are generally recognised as helping to put our immune systems under pressure:

- A poor diet which includes a high proportion of convenience or 'junk' foods
- Regular or excessive alcohol intake
- Smoking
- Insomnia
- Lack of exercise
- Extreme or protracted mental and emotional stress
- Exposure to environmental pollution
- Exercise addiction or eating disorders.

If we recognise the presence of most of these factors in our lives, and suffer from a lack-lustre experience of health, we should set about making positive changes in our lifestyle as soon as possible, in order to replace the basic building blocks for a healthy immune system, and give ourselves a fighting chance of having the most precious gift of all: vibrant health.

The self-defence plan

When we are aiming to stimulate our immune systems into optimum performance, there are four basic areas we need to consider:

- Nutrition and anti-oxidant supplements
- Positive thinking and mental and physical relaxation
- Exercise, hydrotherapy and skin-brushing techniques
- Alternative medical treatment to improve our body's own defence mechanisms.

If our lifestyle is especially stressed and pressured, we may need to implement all these features. Others may find that they only need to concentrate on one or two hitherto neglected areas.

Nutrition and anti-oxidant supplements

You may already be familiar with the phrase 'We are what we eat', and nowhere is this more true than with regard to protecting our body's own defence mechanism. When we eat consistently and well, we are giving our bodies the basic building blocks constantly needed for renewal and repair.

However, apart from ensuring that we generally have a good quality, varied diet high in fresh, whole foods, there are specific nutrients with a particular reputation for supporting our immune systems. These include the anti-oxidant vitamins A, C and E. These 'super nutrients' have been hailed as having the potential to discourage the development of a host of degenerative diseases, including angina, strokes and lung cancer, by boosting our immunity and protecting us against premature ageing. On a day-to-day basis, they may also play a vital role in helping us fight off minor infections by supporting our immune systems.

Free radicals: the secret enemy

Free radicals are an anarchic force in our bodies which interferes with normal cellular activity, causing deterioration and damage. They are created when oxygen is converted into energy (the process of oxidation). Although a certain number are required by the body in order to kill bacteria, when they are produced in excess they may encourage the development of degenerative disease. Free radicals are highly volatile and unstable particles which damage cell membranes and can interfere negatively with genetic material, leading to a 'domino' effect of damage in the body. These cellular rampagers may also be implicated in a worrying range of degenerative illnesses such as heart disease, cancers, rheumatoid arthritis and Parkinson's disease.

Anti-oxidants to the rescue

Although this information is undeniably alarming, the good news is that we can combat some of the negative effects of free radicals on our health by taking some basic positive steps. One of the first and most important of these includes the use of anti-oxidants in our diets. These nutrients have been hailed as playing a central role in the battle against the production of free radicals and their profoundly negative effects on our bodies. Studies of groups deficient in these vitamins have revealed that they are considerably more likely to develop a high level of disease than those who have a significant intake of anti-oxidant nutrients. The latter include beta-carotene (a precursor to vitamin A), vitamin C and vitamin E. If we are serious about limiting the risk of damage from rampaging free radicals, we should also limit our exposure to elements in our lifestyle that can contribute to their production, such as:

• Smoking
• Radiation from the sun
• Atmospheric pollution
• Fried, convenience, or processed foods
• Alcohol

When our bodies are in optimum balance due to a strong inherited constitution and a healthy lifestyle, free radicals are dealt with efficiently by our built-in safety mechanisms. However, if we are exposed daily to atmospheric pollution, extreme stress, cigarette smoke and a poor diet, we are likely to end up with more free radicals circulating in our systems than we can deal with effectively under our own steam. This is where we can call on extra help from anti-oxidants.

Anti-oxidant nutrients fight against the process of oxidation that occurs non-stop in the body. If you want to visualise what the process of oxidation involves, just picture what happens when an apple is cut in half and left to sit for an hour or two. A brown coating develops, the result of the apple reacting with the oxygen in the atmosphere. This degenerative process can also be seen when a car is left in the open air for a long time. Just as the apple reacts to contact with oxygen, so a car chassis will rust and degenerate as a result of a similar process. Although we may not be able to see what is happening, something similar occurs inside our bodies as a result of oxidation and the production of free radicals. Since anti-oxidants are a major tool at our disposal for minimising the damage from oxidation, it makes sense to consider each one in turn in order to grasp how they can help us in the fight for high-level health.

Beta-carotene

Beta-carotene has a twofold function. On the one hand, the body converts it to vitamin A (which is why it is called a precursor to vitamin A); what is left over acts as an anti-oxidant. Foods rich in beta-carotene include fruit and vegetables with a characteristically yellow or orange colour, such as carrots and mangoes. Deep green vegetables such as spinach and broccoli are also a rich source of this nutrient.

Beta-carotene is recognised as one of the most powerful anti-oxidants, because one of its functions is to help prevent fruit and vegetables shrivelling and burning up in the sun. Free radicals are formed in plants as well as humans in response to ultra-violet radiation from the sun, and plants are enabled to survive because of their beta-carotene content. If plants didn't have this in-built form of protection, they wouldn't have a chance of survival. This also has an important application for humans, because beta-carotene supplements can be used to neutralise the damaging effect of sunlight on sensitive skin. Beta-carotene can help protect normal skin from the traumatic effect of strong sunlight, as well as possibly acting as an anti-ageing agent for the skin.

Foods that are rich in beta-carotene include the following: carrots, parsley, sweet potatoes, spinach, watercress, tomatoes, asparagus, broccoli, apricots and peaches. In an ideal situation, we should aim for a daily minimum of five generous portions of beta-carotene-rich fruit and vegetables. Bear in mind also that we can maximise beta-carotene absorption if we take a little fat at the same time. All we need to do is brush vegetables with a sparing amount of cold-pressed, virgin olive oil in order to make the most of our beta-carotene intake.

Unlike vitamin C, beta-carotene remains quite stable during cooking processes. In fact, vegetable sources of this nutrient, such as carrots, have very firm cell walls which must be broken down before the maximum amount of beta-carotene can be released. For this reason, chopped, lightly-puréed, or freshly-juiced vegetables will yield their maximum beta-carotene content for easy absorption by the body.

Vitamin C

It is now generally acknowledged that vitamin C plays an essential role in promoting the growth and repair of body tissue, as well as having a particular affinity with connective tissue in the skin and gums. It also plays a significant role in supporting the efficient functioning of the immune system, and seems to play a key part in helping the body to fight off bacterial and viral infection.

Vitamin C is also a powerful anti-oxidant nutrient which helps us combat the damaging effects of free radicals. It can be found in the fluids that flow between our cells, acting as a 'search and destroy' agent when any roaming free radicals cross its path. However, this can be a difficult vitamin to obtain on a daily basis because it is very easily destroyed on exposure to the air or during the cooking process. As a result, take care when cooking vegetables or fruit to chop them up *just* before cooking, so that their vitamin C content has less chance of oxidising and evaporating into the atmosphere.

Preferred methods of cooking, which preserve the maximum vitamin C content, include steaming, or placing vegetables directly into simmering water, rather than putting them into cold water and waiting until it comes to the boil. The oxidising enzymes that attack vitamin C work less efficiently at high temperatures; when we put chopped vegetables into cold water and bring them to the boil, we destroy twice as much vitamin C.

It is also helpful to simmer vegetables in a small quantity of water which can then be used to make stocks and soups. Quicker methods of cooking are preferable, since it has been estimated that 25 per cent of this vitamin is lost after fifteen minutes of cooking time, while 75 per cent is lost after one and a half hours. Bear in mind storage conditions as well when trying to preserve vitamin C. Newly-dug potatoes have approximately 30 mg of vitamin C in the autumn; this drops to a mere 8 mg by the end of the following spring. For this reason, make an effort to buy vegetables in season and eat all fresh fruit and vegetables soon after purchase in order to maximise your chances of benefiting from their vitamin C content.

Working on the same principle, avoid keeping commercially-produced fruit juices in the fridge for more than four or five days after opening, because the vitamin C content may have been as much as halved by this time. Also avoid shaking a container of juice, since this encourages contact with oxygen and diminishes the vitamin C content even further. Foods containing vitamin C include the following: blackcurrants, parsley, raw green peppers, strawberries, watercress, sprouts, lemons, oranges, broccoli, grapefruit and cauliflower.

Vitamin E

Vitamin E has been hailed as the most important anti-oxidant due to its potential for protecting the fats that surround every cell in our bodies. It is also of vital importance in maintaining the efficient working of our immune systems because of the way it can strengthen white blood cells against infection. It has also been suggested that vitamin E plays an important role in discouraging disease and deterioration of the heart and circulatory system. Because vitamin E works by preventing fats from turning rancid in the body, it plays a central role in protecting the layer of fatty tissue that covers our major organs. In addition, it prevents the fats we may ingest, such as vegetable oil, from 'going off' once inside the body. As a result, we need to increase the amount of vitamin E that we consume in proportion to the amount of polyunsaturated fat (such as solid sunflower oil spreads) we eat.

Vitamin E appears to work in tandem with vitamin C in neutralising free radicals in the body, so it is important to make sure that we have optimum quantities of both vitamins in our diet. It has been suggested that the most effective form of vitamin E is to found in natural sources such as soya bean or wheat germ oil. It is also possible to obtain synthetic vitamin E made from petrochemicals, but it has been estimated that this is approximately 36 per cent less effective than natural vitamin E. Natural sources can be identified by the prefixed letter 'd' (such as d-alpha tocopherol) while synthetic sources are prefixed with 'dl' (such as dl-alpha tocopherol).

Vitamin E is obtained mainly from vegetable oils (wheat germ, sunflower, or safflower), nuts and whole grains. However, it is very easily lost through any form of processing such as the refining of white flour. Vitamin E also suffers when it comes into contact with oxygen in the air, warmth, or sunlight. As a result, vegetable oils should be stored in a cool, dark cupboard or fridge with the stopper firmly secured.

As with vitamin C, cooking methods can also compromise vitamin E content; deep frying and deep freezing cause the major problems. Frying is a particular hazard, because up to 90 per cent of vitamin E can be lost, especially if the cooking oil has become rancid.

Do we need supplements or not?

Now that we know the valuable part played by anti-oxidant enzymes in protecting optimum levels of health, we come to the inevitable question: 'Is it possible to obtain enough of these vitamins from our diet, or must we use vitamin supplements in order to ensure that we are getting enough?' For the basic arguments for and against vitamin supplements, see Chapter Three ('Nutritional Boosters').

Positive thinking

Many of us are already aware of the profound effect our state of mind can have on our general health and well-being. An obvious example of this two-way process is the minor illness which often develops following a period of emotional stress. In other words coping with demanding or negative events for an extended period of time can exhaust us physically, as well as leaving us open to minor infections. We may also be familiar with the pattern of stress-related chronic conditions such as migraine or Irritable Bowel Syndrome where stress can trigger an acute episode of the problem.

Interestingly, we are less likely to experience symptoms when the stress factors are at their height; more often than not, they occur when the strain has been relieved and we have begun to relax a little. It may seem infuriating or bewildering to be suffering symptoms at the very point when stress has been dealt with, but the situation begins to make more sense if we regard the emergence of acute symptoms as the body's way of taking time out in order to recover.

Further exploration into the mind/body link is being carried out in the field of psychoneuroimmunology. Information from this relatively new but developing field of scientific enquiry draws attention to the profound way our thoughts can influence the functioning of our immune systems and the quality of our overall health. A recent study conducted at the University of Reading revealed that subjects who deliberately recalled positive memories had elevated immune antibodies when their saliva samples were tested before and after this recall. In contrast, those who induced a negative or guilt-ridden mood were found to have depressed antibodies.

The results of similar studies suggest that experiencing pleasurable sensations and looking back on positive events may play an important role in keeping our health on track. However, it has also been revealed that in order to boost our potential for maximum immunity we need to keep these positive experiences 'topped up' at fairly regular intervals. This is because, although we appear to get a fairly immediate boost to our immune system from a happy event, positive influence on antibody production requires us to keep our emotional needs well supplied.

Sensual pleasures also play their part in boosting high-level immunity, according to studies conducted at the University of Westminster. The level of the immune antibody SIgA in saliva was measured in subjects before, during and after smelling a range of pleasant or repellent odours including chocolate, water and rotten meat. The conclusion was that attractive odours boosted immune antibody levels, while offensive smells suppressed this response for roughly half an hour after exposure to the odour.

Studies of this kind suggest that our health can benefit greatly from managing stress as effectively as we can through pampering ourselves at regular intervals. Giving ourselves time to relax and unwind, read a favourite novel, watch an enjoyable film, have a laugh with friends, soak in an aromatic bath, and treat ourselves to a massage are all ways that we can look after our emotional and physical well-being.

Exercise and skin-brushing techniques

See the section on 'Exercise and the immune system' on p. 99 for general advice on the positive impact that keeping physically fit can have on immune system performance.

Skin-brushing techniques and lymphatic stimulation

As we will discover in the Exercise Boosters chapter, we are dependent on the efficient flow of lymphatic fluid through our bodies to eliminate toxins, transport nutrients to our tissues and, above all, help our immune systems to work smoothly and well. The following are all persuasive reasons for doing all we can to protect our lymphatic systems:

• Because our immune systems rely upon the efficient working of our lymph systems, keeping the latter in good order helps our bodies fight disease and recurrent infections

- Fatigue and lethargy are less likely to be a problem
- Early ageing as a result of cell degeneration may be postponed
- The risk of developing cellulite is minimised.

Once we recognise how dependent we are on a healthy, efficient lymphatic system in order to look and feel our best, it makes tremendously good sense to take those constructive and positive steps which are reputed to support its smooth functioning.

Dry skin-brushing techniques are claimed to be one of the most 'hands on', direct and effective ways of stimulating drainage of lymphatic fluid. All you need is to use a natural bristle brush each day to brush your skin before showering or bathing. The brush should be used in large sweeping movements which cover your body, moving in a downward direction to the trunk and upwards from the feet, legs and hips.

Avoid using too much pressure at first, especially if you are generally unfit and not in great shape: just settle for the amount of pressure that feels comfortable to you. Also avoid brushing any areas of skin that are damaged or irritated, or where there are clusters of broken veins: these areas should always be treated gently and with caution. Don't be tempted to overdo skin brushing, you only need to brush your whole body once a day in order to achieve the optimum effect of eliminating toxic waste and stimulating lymphatic drainage.

Elimination of cellulite

Skin brushing has the additional advantage of being one of the most effective means at our disposal of dealing with cellulite (the bumpy skin with the appearance of orange peel that has a tendency to appear on hips, thighs, upper arms and belly). The pitted texture of cellulite is thought to reveal the stagnant nature of the affected tissues, with toxic waste building up as a result of inefficient circulation and inefficient flow of lymphatic fluid.

In addition to being a cosmetic drawback, the presence of cellulite is also thought to be a physical indication that our systems are not eliminating toxic waste as efficiently as they should. As a result, those of us who suffer severely from cellulite often find that we experience problems with recurrent lethargy and fatigue due to a sluggish, over-toxic system.

Additional ways of dealing with cellulite include the following.

Exercise

Low-intensity, regular aerobic exercise taken three or four times a week stimulates circulation, improves the potential of the body for absorbing and utilising oxygen and stimulates the flow of lymphatic fluid. All these factors are of central importance in any plan aimed at reducing the production, or improving the appearance, of cellulite. As with any other exercise plan, always choose a form of exercise that appeals to your temperament in order to give yourself the best chance of continuing with enthusiasm. Possible exercise options include cycling, dancing, brisk walking, skiing, or rowing. The time spent exercising should ideally leave us feeling physically and men- tally energised rather than exhausted.

It is also important to put a premium on the regularity of our exercise routine, in order to gain maximum benefit from it. In other words, it is better to set aside time for three sessions of physical activity each week, rather than put it off and then spend a couple of hours at the gym every two or three weeks.

Eating the right foods

Foods to be avoided because they encourage cellulite include any items containing a hefty proportion of white sugar, animal fat (such as cream and butter), red meat, coffee, tea, alcohol and salt. Dietary allies in our fight against cellulite production include fresh fruit, raw vegetables, whole grains, mineral water and small proportions of additive-free poultry, eggs and fish if we aren't vegetarian. It is also claimed that kelp and sea vegetables such as seaweed can play a valuable part in discouraging cellulite production.

Avoiding crash diets

Always avoid the temptation of crash or yo-yo dieting, since these extreme patterns of dietary restriction encourage fatigue and exhaustion. In addition, weight-loss plans have been shown to do very little to help stabilise our weight at a healthy, steady level.

Sadly, the reverse is often true, because many of us who are on a perpetual diet discover that pounds refuse to budge after a while and, once we return to a normal eating pattern, they go back on again with disturbing and depressing rapidity. What is worse, it has been suggested that if we are prone to fluctuating, unstable levels of weight, we are at great risk of making our problems with cellulite worse, as well as contributing to extra risk of stretch marks.

Cellulite production is particularly increased by a vicious circle of weight loss and weight gain, because drastic diets encourage the breaking down of muscle tissue in the body. Unfortunately, this is replaced by fatty tissue which has a reputation for contributing to the formation of cellulite. Being on a diet that drastically reduces calories at the expense of the nutritional quality of the food eaten also deprives the body of essential nutrients, needed to prevent or arrest the formation of cellulite. This is made even worse if we are prone to rapid fluctuations of weight and don't keep our muscles well-toned through regular exercise.

Baths

When taking a bath always make sure it isn't too hot, and also avoid wearing clothes that are very tight around the waist, hips and thighs, which can interfere with circulation: both can be co-factors in contributing to cellulite production.

Lymphatic drainage massage

Lymphatic drainage massage (LDM) has also been hailed as an effective way of stimulating the lymph system, improving the performance of the immune system and aiding in the reduction of cellulite. In addition, the following problems may also be improved by LDM: water retention, muscle tension, poor-quality skin, lethargy and generally poor resistance to minor illnesses and infections. LDM acts by stimulating the flow of lymph and blood through slow pumping movements, aiding the body's cleansing and detoxifying functions.

Hydrotherapy

Hydrotherapy techniques have also been recommended by naturopaths for years as a way of improving immune system performance. In addition, regular use of simple hydrotherapy techniques at home can be invaluable for invigorating our bodies and improving skin tone and texture.

Because water is such a basic element in our lives, it is very easy for us to take it for granted and overlook the importance of its role for our well-being. Bear in mind that we can survive without food for an astonishingly long period of time, but once we are deprived of water we will die very rapidly indeed. Dehydration can be a serious complication in illness, especially where a lot of fluid is lost quickly, as in cases where vomiting and diarrhoea occur together. This risk is even greater in young children or the elderly, because dehydration can be fatal if it is not arrested promptly by replacing vital fluid.

Our general affinity with water as an element becomes even clearer if we consider that our bodies are made up of more than 70 per cent water. We are dependent on the free circulation of this essential liquid for the smooth maintenance of basic bodily functions. Once we are deprived of adequate supplies of water we stop eliminating waste matter from our bodies, with the attendant risk of a fatal build-up of toxic matter within our systems.

Thus, water plays a role of central importance in ensuring our survival on a physiological level, but it can also play a very positive role in stimulating a sense of physical, emotional, and mental well-being when applied within the context of hydrotherapy techniques.

The use of water as a therapeutic agent in supporting the healing process is not new: spa towns in Britain and Europe based the success of their claims on the positive effect on health of 'taking the waters'. Spa water was purported to have beneficial effects when drunk or bathed in, for a range of health problems that could affect the skin and internal organs.

Many of the techniques employed today at popular spa resorts were originally devised by Sebastian Kneipp in the nineteenth century. Treatments may involve the use of sea water (Thalassotherapy) or fresh water (Hydrotherapy) and it is claimed that they convey a wide range of health benefits, such as:

- The improvement of sluggish circulation
- Increased vitality
- Greater protection against illness and skin conditions
- Improvement in skin tone and texture
- Improved mucous membrane function and reduction in catarrh, as the elimination of toxins is encouraged through the skin rather than through the mucous membranes
- Better bowel, lung and kidney function as the skin takes on a more efficient eliminative role
- Reduction of cellulite.

Some of Kneipp's hydrotherapy techniques may be used at home, but this option should only be considered if you are in good health with no history of circulatory problems (heart disease, angina, varicose veins, or high blood pressure), diabetes, or a chronic skin condition (such as eczema or psoriasis). If there is any doubt, you should always consult your GP or alternative health practitioner before embarking on any course of action that might carry a potential health risk.

When using simple hydrotherapy techniques at home, the following hints should always be borne in mind:

- Never apply cold water to your skin when chilled. Always warm up first by taking a warm shower or doing some gentle exercise.
- Use cold water for a maximum of thirty seconds, building up to this slowly if it feels too much at first.
- If there is any feeling of uneasiness about using cold water at the outset, start by using warm water and alternating with cold.
- After finishing your hydrotherapy session, to obtain maximum benefit leave damp areas to dry naturally rather than towelling

your whole body. In other words, only dry the areas that will not be covered by clothing.

- Make a point of generating body heat after cold treatments by taking a brisk short walk, or resting in bed after a warm treatment.
- Hydrotherapy treatments at spa resorts use custom-made high power water jets that can be directed at specific parts of the body that need treatment such as the hips, thighs, and buttocks in order to stimulate circulation. A reasonable substitute at home can be obtained by using a hand-held domestic shower.
- Begin treatment by taking a comfortably warm shower. Switch to cold for about twenty seconds, back to warm and then finally to cold again.
- A stimulating effect can be obtained by moving a hand-held shower spray down the body, starting with the face and moving down the arms, chest, stomach and legs.
- Cold water treatments can be used in relation to a specific part of the body in order to tone up the skin in that area. A good example of this technique would include spraying the breasts with cold water in order to enhance the smoothness and firmness of breast tissue. An alternative method involves using two flannels and bowls of warm and cold water. Apply a hot wrung-out flannel to one breast until it is fully warmed. Alternate this with the application of a cold flannel prepared in the same way. Treat each breast in turn, using three applications of heat and cold and always making sure that the cycle ends with using a cool flannel.

Bathing

Taking a leisurely bath can be an invaluable way of promoting relaxation, resting the mind and body and soothing tense or aching muscles. Luxuriating in a warm, fragrant bath will not have the stimulating or invigorating effect of the hydrotherapy techniques mentioned above, but it can play a significant part in aiding the process of detoxification, especially if seaweed or mud preparations are used before or during bathing. In order to obtain maximum benefit from bathing, it helps to observe the following hints:

- Essential oils can be added to the bath water in order to complement or re-balance your mood. Possible soothing oils to consider include lavender, camomile, rose or geranium. On the other hand, an uplifting or stimulating bath can be created by using sandalwood, tangerine or grapefruit. Bear in mind that essential oils are extremely concentrated; very few drops are needed in the bath water, usually no more than five to six drops.

- Avoid taking baths that are very hot: the ideal temperature should not be above 36–38 degrees centigrade (97–100 degrees Fahrenheit). If the water is too hot, the overall effect is likely to be enervating rather than refreshing. Additional problems that can follow from taking too hot a bath include raised blood pressure, cellulite and broken veins.

- Use an exfoliating preparation on damp skin before getting into your bath. Areas of skin to concentrate on include elbows, hips, buttocks, thighs, knees and heels. Exfoliating these areas will refine the texture of the skin on these parts of the body, while at the same time encouraging more efficient absorption of the essential oils or detoxifying preparations that may be used in the bath water. Alternatively, a skin conditioning and detoxifying seaweed cream can be applied to the skin immediately after getting out of the bath, while the skin is warm and receptive.

- Seaweed products can be dissolved in the bath water, or a mud treatment can be applied to the skin before showering. Both seaweed and mud have a reputation for cleansing and detoxifying properties. Baths should never be hotter than tepid or warm if powdered seaweed is being added. The reason for this is simple: a very hot seaweed bath is overwhelmingly stimulating, and can cause uncomfortable sensations of palpitations, and a rapid heartbeat. Bearing this in mind, anyone with a history of high blood pressure or circulatory problems should avoid experimenting with seaweed preparations.

Boosting the body's defences by alternative medical treatment

Alternative medical systems such as homoeopathy or traditional Chinese medicine are aptly called 'alternative' medical systems because they really do provide us with a perspective that is radically different to the conventional medical approach.

Conventional medicine dictates that our bodies are rather like machines made up of specialised and intricate parts that can function well in times of good health, but can be subject to malfunction as a result of a number of factors. The ageing process, with its attendant problems of 'wear and tear', is seen as a particularly strong reason for problems occurring with various organs and structures in the body such as bones and joints. In addition, exposure to specific infective agents, or physical trauma, are also seen as potential triggers for serious problems with our overall health. Conventional doctors are also accepting more diffuse precipitating dynamics such as stress, or additional lifestyle factors such as an unhealthy or unbalanced diet, excess of alcohol or smoking.

Most treatments, however, concentrate on isolating the specific drug (often referred to as the 'magic bullet') designed to neutralise the specific bacterium, inflammatory response, or chemical imbalance that may be causing a problem. Unfortunately, although a great deal of time and effort is put into trying to develop drugs with as specific an action as possible on a targeted area, undesirable side-effects often arise in other systems of the body in response to strong conventional drugs such as antibiotics, anti-inflammatories, or steroids. This can sometimes set off a chain reaction where additional drugs are needed to off-set the negative effects of a drug, which can lead to further side-effects of their own. This is a particularly worrying problem when certain orthodox drugs such as steroids are known to depress the immune system.

A more holistic approach to healing, however, tends to place more emphasis on what makes us susceptible to illness, rather than being absorbed in finding the specific magic bullet. As a result, if recurrent infections are a problem, an alternative therapist will probably want to explore ways of supporting the body's own capacity to fight off infection more effectively. This may take the form of investigating stress-reduction techniques if susceptibility to recurrent minor infection seems to have followed a period of protracted stress (which, as we have seen above, can have a marked adverse effect on compromising the performance of the immune system). In addition, improving the natural defences of the body can include improving general nutritional status, or using specific treatments known to increase the body's resistance to infection.

Is an alternative medical approach suitable for my problems?

If you answer 'yes' to more than one of the following questions, you might benefit considerably from a course of alternative treatment such as Western medical herbalism, homoeopathy, naturopathy, or traditional Chinese medicine.

- Do you suffer from more than one cold a year?
- Do you have a history of recurrent cystitis or thrush?
- Do you have mysterious skin reactions that come and go at recurrent intervals (these could include redness, dryness, or generally irritating patches of skin)?
- Do you suffer from cold sores when you are run down?
- Do you have generally poor skin quality, with a tendency for your skin to 'break out' in boils or large spots?
- Do you have episodes of pain or stiffness in the small joints of your fingers and toes?
- Do the glands feel swollen in your neck or armpits from time to time?
- Do you suffer from persistently low energy levels, with difficulty in accomplishing all the tasks you need to do professionally and at home?

Natural alternatives to antibiotics

Any of the following can be used as 'first resort' treatment for acute, limited infections such as cystitis, colds, sore throats, coughs, or thrush. However, if symptoms do not respond promptly or appear to build in severity, seek professional medical help for further advice in managing the condition. Also bear in mind that drugs such as steroids should never be withdrawn without careful medical supervision and support.

Garlic

Various important properties have been attributed to garlic, including its natural qualities as an antibiotic and nourisher of the immune system. It has also been suggested that it can act as an anti-viral and anti-fungal agent, stimulating the gut to work in a more efficient and balanced way. This is in sharp contrast to conventional antibiotics, which can have an adverse effect by disturbing the delicate balance of the intestinal flora. Although raw garlic can be included in the diet, it is difficult to eat the quantities needed to have a therapeutic effect and keep an active social or romantic life! Instead, it is more practical to opt for tablets made from a high concentration of powdered garlic. These can now be obtained in one-a-day formulae to be taken for as long as the infection continues. Alternatively, if there is a past history of chest problems in the winter, a prophylactic dose may be taken from early autumn to spring.

Cranberry

Cranberry juice has a particularly strong reputation for reducing the incidence of urinary tract infections such as cystitis, due to an ingredient that discourages bacteria from lodging in the bladder and urinary tract. Cranberry should be taken as tablets or juice at the first twinge of uneasiness in the bladder; drink liberal quantities of water with it in order to flush out the urinary tract. If you have a history of cystitis, a small glass of cranberry juice can be taken daily to discourage infection developing in the first place.

Aloe vera

Hailed as a powerful antiseptic and enhancer of the immune system, aloe vera is thought to be especially effective in supporting the body's defences in dealing with stomach bugs and upsets. It can be taken in the form of juice or tablets for internal use, and can also be used externally in the form of a gel as a topical antiseptic or soothing agent for minor burns.

Echinacea

This is considered a powerful ally in supporting our bodies in fighting viral infections such as colds, flu and related secondary complications such as sinusitis. Echinacea appears to act as a catalyst in supporting the immune system in fighting the virus that is causing the problem. It can be obtained in tincture or tablet form; approximately fifteen drops of tincture need to be taken three times a day in a small amount of water. Instructions for the optimum dosage for the tablets should be included on the packaging. Echinacea probably acts most effectively when taken at the first sign of infection, and it should be continued for as long as symptoms persist. However, it is apparently not as effective when taken as a prophylactic against infection.

Oscillococcinum

This is one of the very few homoeopathic remedies that is a specific treatment for a specific condition: most homoeopathic remedies are selected on the basis of an analysis of the individual symptoms of each patient. However, oscillococcinum appears to be an effective first resort in treating any patients who are suffering from cold or flu symptoms. When taken in the initial, feverish stage of illness, oscillococcinum appears to stimulate the immune system to fight the cold or flu virus more effectively than it might do under its own steam. As a result, symptoms should be less severe and more short-lived, and there should be a reduced risk of complications. The remedy is taken in tablet form and can be obtained from a homoeo-pathic pharmacy.

Grapefruit seed extract

Grapefruit seed extract is thought to have antibiotic, anti-viral and anti-fungal properties and is especially recommended for throat infection and stomach bugs. It comes in tablet or liquid form and ten drops of the extract may be taken twice or three times a day while symptoms persist.

Licorice

Substantial claims have been made for licorice's ability to act as a tonic for the immune system when it has been suppressed by a period of stress, or by taking conventional medication such as steroids. It has been suggested that it is especially helpful in assisting the body in fighting throat infections, thrush, or cold sores. Dosage should begin as soon as symptoms appear; take two to ten capsules a day, or follow the manufacturer's instructions.

Elderberry extract

Elderberry extract appears to have a powerful inhibiting effect on the spread of viruses, and it is claimed that it can stimulate recovery from flu within three days. It can be taken in lozenge or liquid form to treat viral infections, chest infections and heavy colds or flu.

Tea tree oil

This essential oil has a strong reputation as a protection against a range of viral, bacterial and fungal infections. It should not be taken internally, but used as an external treatment by adding four drops to a foot bath in order to soothe athlete's foot, or six to eight drops to a hip bath in order to ease symptoms of thrush and cystitis.

For additional suggestions for supporting the immune system in fighting infection and maintaining high-grade health, see the section on recurrent infections on p. 165 in the 'Quick-fix' section (Chapter Six).

3

Nutritional Boosters

The whole question of how to eat well has become a minefield of contradictions for many of us. We are bombarded with nutritional advice from such a variety of directions that it is often difficult to make much sense of it all. Should we eat butter, margarine, or solid olive-oil type spreads? Should we seriously consider becoming vegetarian if we really want to enjoy the greatest potential for good health? Do we have to eat only organic foods if we want to get the maximum nutritional benefit? And what about produce that has been genetically modified? These are just a few of the questions for which we might want no-nonsense answers.

In this section of the six-point plan, we shall try to cut through this confusion by approaching the whole issue of healthy eating from a realistic perspective. It would all be so easy if we lived in an ideal world where we had infinite amounts of time for growing our own organic vegetables and cooking balanced meals from scratch using only the finest ingredients, or could spend hours keeping up with the latest nutritional information. Unfortunately, for the majority of us this can't happen because we have to work within the realistic framework of busy jobs, the tastes and preferences of family members, budgetary constraints and the boredom thresholds that demand that food should not be spartan or lacking in flavour, texture, or variety.

Most importantly, we need to appreciate that food has a significance in our lives that goes far beyond issues of nutrition and providing physical sustenance. As a result, we need to explore some of these basic areas if we are to understand our relationship with food. By doing so, we are less likely to fall into the common trap of trying to take on board an eating plan that is inappropriate to our physical and psychological needs. This is why so many attempts at starting a healthy new diet fail after a very short time. On the other hand, once we understand some of the psychological aspects of our complex relationship with food, we have an important base-line to work from before we even start talking about specific foods and their merits and demerits.

The psychological minefield of nutrition

Eating is about so much more than providing building materials and energy sources for our bodies. What, how much, and how we eat can have a great deal to do with broader aspects of pleasure, sensuality and issues of control and power. Eating disorders, for example, have much more to do with self-image and our psychological well-being (or lack of it) than simple questions of nutrition. As a result, we can force-feed an anorexic patient in an effort to provide them with the essential fluid and nutritional building blocks their body requires, but this will not help them come to terms with the psychological problems that are compelling them to reduce their intake of food drastically in the first place. Until this is done, meaningful progress is unlikely to happen.

The roots of our complex relationship with food can be found in the way that our parents rewarded or punished us by giving or withholding food 'treats'. This early formative experience can be partly responsible for the guilt that many of us feel in relation to certain foods, drinks, or eating patterns. This residual guilt can, in turn, also be reinforced in diet plans where some foods are referred to as 'sins' or 'indulgences'. Once we have taken this insidious perspective on board, we are not very likely to develop a healthy or balanced attitude towards food in general. This is very significant because the latest approaches to healthy weight loss have come to the conclusion that we are far more inclined to reach our optimum weight when we relax about our daily food intake and become more concerned with the nutritional status of food rather than its 'fattening' or 'non-fattening' status.

As a result, we must ensure that any positive changes we make in our eating patterns make allowances for the fact that we need to get a significant amount of sensual pleasure from what we eat. Put simply, this means that we shall have a much greater chance of sticking to whatever dietary changes we make. On the other hand, the moment we push ourselves to take on board dietary changes which make us feel deprived or punished, we are less likely to succeed in maintaining our good intentions. There is the subtler additional risk that we may begin to enjoy depriving ourselves and become attached to a spartan approach to eating which is too exclusive and may cost us dearly in terms of our social life.

Because of the importance of this psychological dimension, the advice given in this chapter works from the basic premise that we should be trying to include more nutritious and delicious foods in our daily intake. This is in sharp contrast to other eating plans, which spend most of their time making us feel guilty by telling us what to remove from our diets, without replacing these favourite foods with viable alternatives.

It will also become clear as we move through this chapter that what is being proposed is a realistic change of eating habits. In other words, this change does not require us to take drastic steps that we cannot maintain if we have a job that involves regularly eating out, family pressures that make a restrictive diet unworkable, or a busy social life that gives us a great deal of pleasure and fun.

Our aim in this section is to get the basic framework in place so that our eating patterns are essentially sound and healthy. There will be times when we shall need to become more vigilant about getting things right (if we have been through a period of extended stress, for example, or are recovering from a bout of illness), in order to boost ourselves back to optimum levels of health. However, there will also be the phases (when we are on holiday, going through an especially exciting time at work, or when we just want to take a relaxed and leisurely approach to life) when we can apply this basic advice and still allow ourselves enough slack to have fun.

The crucial importance of sound nutrition

We cannot overestimate the importance of the quality of the food we eat every day. If we consume junk foods over an extended period of time, we are likely to find our energy levels flagging, begin to notice the emergence of minor but persistent digestive problems, and our appearance will eventually mirror this lacklustre level of health and vitality through poor-quality skin, hair and nails.

Of course we always hear about those amazing exceptions to the rule, who smoke sixty cigarettes a day, sleep a couple of hours a night, eat fish and chips and fast foods until the cows come home and appear to be fine. However, although this may be true in the short term, there is a strong chance that they will begin to show signs of strain when their energy reserves are eventually used up. It is also important to bear in mind that an average person with a less vigorous constitution is likely to show these symptoms much sooner, in a general state of health that is lacking in sparkle and vitality.

Before we get too depressed by this, it is important to realise that we can reverse the picture and over a long period reap the positive benefits of meeting our daily dietary requirements. These benefits are obvious and wide-ranging and will probably include the following: higher and more stable energy levels, smoother and more efficient digestion, improved texture of skin, hair and nails, fewer niggling aches and pains, and a reduction in mood swings.

This gives us an inkling of the fundamental importance of sound nutrition to our well-being, and the profound impact its presence or absence can have on the overall quality of our lives. Having acknowledged the essential importance of our nutritional status, how can we continue to ignore the quality of what we eat?

Basic boundaries

Eating for energy

If we want to have optimum energy levels, it is essential that we consider the quality of what we eat regularly. Of course, as we have discussed elsewhere, making sure that we have regular exercise and good quality sleep also plays an important role in promoting healthy supplies of energy, but if our diet remains poor we shall only be able to achieve limited overall results. On the other hand, if we make a healthy diet our priority and combine this with optimum amounts of restful sleep and enjoyable, stimulating exercise, we shall have hit on a winning formula that will give us the extra stamina and vitality we need to meet our professional and personal goals each day.

Essential energy foods

These are the foods that should ideally form the backbone of our daily diet in order to ensure maximum levels of optimum energy release. If they seem to be deficient in your diet, introduce them every day, building up the quantity and regularity steadily and slowly.

Raw, fresh fruit and vegetables
Try to include as many portions as possible during the day, putting particular emphasis on dark green vegetables and plenty of red and orange fruit. These will give you the best chance of meeting your needs for anti-oxidant nutrients and vitamin C to increase your immune system's performance and protect you against premature ageing, with its attendant risk of degenerative disease. Fruit and

vegetables are also a valuable source of dietary fibre which helps protect us against constipation and heart disease. Eat fruit and vegetables raw as often as possible, as this is less likely to reduce the vitamin C content.

Cold-pressed, virgin olive oil

When choosing an oil for use in stir-frying, opt for cold-pressed olive oil, which appears to have essential properties which protect our circulatory systems (unlike animal fats or hydrogenated vegetable oils, which seem to do the reverse). Salad dressings should be made from cold-pressed sunflower or safflower oil. Try to keep your fat consumption to within 20 per cent of your overall dietary intake; we eat far too much fat in the Western world and this has serious implications for our health (including increased risks of heart disease and certain cancers such as prostate cancer).

Whole grains, wholemeal products and complex carbohydrates

Whole grains (brown rice, oats, rye and buckwheat) are an essential source of complex carbohydrates, along with pulses and starchy vegetables such as potatoes. These complex carbohydrates are a vital source of essential nutrients (complete proteins are formed by combining pulses with grains such as brown rice) and also provide us with slow-release carbohydrates to sustain our energy levels. Many of us are under the illusion that we should avoid carbohydrates such as wholemeal bread, pasta or potatoes because they are fattening. However, what is often overlooked is that it is not the bread or pasta that is the health hazard, but the fatty spreads or sauces that are added to them.

Small servings of low-fat protein

Small helpings of free-range chicken or fish can play a valuable role in providing variety, flavour and texture to a diet that can otherwise rather lack interest. They can also provide an additional source of essential protein for building and repairing body cells, while helping us avoid the high saturated fat content of red meats such as beef.

Oily fish also plays an important role in protecting the health of our hearts and circulatory systems through the presence of omega 3 fatty acids. Rich sources include herrings, mackerel and fresh salmon. Tinned fish eaten with the bones (sardines and tinned salmon) also provides an important source of calcium in the diet. On the other hand, always remember when cooking chicken to remove the skin beforehand. Not only is there a high proportion of saturated fat in the skin, but removing the skin also allows more fat to run out during the cooking process.

Fruit and herb teas

Many us may have been thoroughly put off drinking herbal teas or grain coffees by disastrous experiences in the past with dandelion coffee and camomile tea. Thankfully the days are past when these were the only available alternatives to regular tea or coffee, since there are now increasingly imaginative and enticing blends of herb, fruit, or grain coffees and teas on the market. Fruit teas can have the tart, refreshing taste of citrus fruit, the sweetness of strawberries, or the exotic taste of spices such as cinnamon. Once you have found an enjoyable range of flavours, rotate them in order to avoid the temptation to take too much too often of one herb. The occasional cup of Chinese green tea is refreshing and stimulating, as well as having additional anti-oxidant properties that appear to help our bodies cope with fat metabolism.

Water

Although it may seem to be stating the obvious, it is vitally important to drink regular quantities of filtered water or still mineral water daily. When storing mineral water in plastic bottles, always avoid leaving them on a shelf near a window. This is important because exposure to sunlight can encourage leaching of chemicals from the plastic container into the water. The best way of solving this problem is to opt instead for water sold in glass containers. It is also a good idea to read the labels of bottled water in order to check that sodium levels are not too high (these waters tend to have a characteristically salty flavour). This is especially relevant if you suffer from high blood pressure, or additional circulatory problems.

Some of us may mistakenly believe that we are taking enough fluid during the day because we have a cup of tea or coffee at frequent intervals. Unfortunately, other health considerations aside, tea and coffee have diuretic (water eliminating) properties, with the result that they encourage the body to excrete fluid. Benefits from increasing the daily amount of water we drink include improved appearance and texture of the skin, as toxins are flushed more efficiently from the body. Anyone who suffers from a history of recurrent cystitis or kidney infections should also make a point of drinking water regularly through the day in order to flush out the urinary system. Bear in mind that dehydration is the commonest trigger for constipation.

Energy draining foods

The best way of eliminating as many energy-reducing foods as possible from our diets is slowly and steadily to replace them with some of the alternatives mentioned above. So, if we enjoy pasta, we can use up our existing stock of refined pasta and when it has gone replace it with a wholemeal variety. In this way the transition to an energising diet can be made smoothly and cumulatively.

High-fat foods

The main offenders are foods that are high in saturated fat, such as red meat, full-fat milk, hard cheeses (cheddar), and butter. Eggs should also be used sparingly because of their high cholesterol content, despite the fact that they are good sources of calcium and protein. If dairy foods are a particular favourite and the thought of drastically cutting them down seems impossible, bear in mind that there are some basic strategies we can use to minimise the damage. One of the most effective is to make sure that we include regular portions of soluble fibre in our diets from a vegetable source such as peas and beans. In addition, remember that the adverse effect of saturated fat on the body appears to be increased when we eat a high proportion of foods that combine sugar with saturated fat (such as cakes, biscuits or ice cream). So if we do like to eat full-fat cheeses from time to time, we should make it a priority to stay away from these sorts of sweets.

Refined carbohydrates

These are easily identified as foods that have been stripped of a large part of their nutritional value through an aggressive refining process. Foods that fall into this category include white flour, white sugar, white rice and any products made from these raw ingredients such as white bread. All these foods are nutritionally bereft and a source of 'empty' calories. This means that if we include a high proportion of these refined foods in our diet we will use up essential nutrients in the process of metabolism (the burning up of food in order to release energy), that will not be adequately replaced by the food taken in. This is why many of us whose diet includes a very high proportion of refined foods high in sugar may find that we gain a great deal of weight and suffer from a form of low-grade malnutrition. Also bear in mind that one of the most common sources of 'hidden' refined sugar is found in fizzy drinks and tinned foods. If not adding sugar is difficult, don't reach for artificial sweeteners (which can cause other health problems of their own, such as an increased risk of developing allergies), try using molasses instead. This is a form of unrefined sugar cane extract that has a sweetness of its own while also providing traces of minerals and vitamins. Although an acquired taste at first, it can become quite palatable as it becomes familiar.

Processed, 'instant' foods

Convenience foods are very useful when time is tight, but they do bring their own problems because of the presence of ingredients such as chemical additives, preservatives, colourings and flavourings such as sodium. Although necessary in small amounts, too much sodium can cause severe problems, leading to an imbalance between sodium and potassium in the body. Unfortunately, commercially prepared foods also tend to include significant amounts of sugar and fat, which make them a potential health hazard when eaten regularly.

The nutritional situation can be made even worse when meals with a high content of sugar, fat and chemical additive have been sitting in the deep freeze for two to three months before being microwaved. Although it may be necessary from time to time to make use of convenience foods, it is possible to do a 'damage limitation' exercise by following a few simple steps listed below in the 'Trouble-shooting strategies' section.

Coffee and tea

These need to be used in strict moderation only, especially if we enjoy these drinks most when they are very strong. A range of unpleasant symptoms can result from over-frequent consumption of coffee and tea, including poor sleep patterns, palpitations, nausea, indigestion, headaches and irritability. In addition, heavy coffee and tea consumption can reduce our ability to absorb vitamin C and iron, while encouraging calcium to leach from our bones (putting us at greater risk of developing osteoporosis). However, it is very important not to do anything drastic when cutting down the amount of strong tea and coffee you drink, because this can lead to symptoms of caffeine withdrawal very similar to the features of caffeine addiction listed above, with protracted and severe headaches. So we need to be very realistic when we set about giving up or strictly reducing our intake of tea and coffee. Cut intake down slowly and steadily by substituting decaffeinated tea or coffee, coffee substitute, or green or herbal teas for the fully caffeinated variety at a rate of one cup a day. By doing it this way, the transition away from caffeinated drinks should be as smooth and painless as possible.

Alcohol

Although it has some positive health-giving benefits in moderate amounts (a small glass of red wine a day is thought to have beneficial effects on the heart and circulatory system), too much of a good thing can cause a host of problems. Too high or too frequent a consumption of alcohol can leave us vulnerable to health problems including liver damage, osteoporosis, signs of premature ageing and violent changes of mood. In order to avoid these pitfalls, we need to adopt a healthy approach in managing how much we drink. This is especially relevant to women because they have a higher proportion of body fat than men. As a result, the lean tissue in their bodies tends to become flooded with alcohol more rapidly than that of a man, because fat cells do not take up alcohol due to their limited blood supply. Women may also be aware that they are more sensitive to the adverse effect of alcohol on their emotional well-being around the time of their periods. This often manifests itself in more severe swings of mood and a general tendency to feel down and depressed, because alcohol is a chemical depressant and mood enhancer. One of the best ways of managing our alcohol intake is to be aware of the maximum recommended allowance and to make a point of staying well within it. Men should have no more than twenty-one units of alcohol a week, and women should stay within fourteen units. A unit is the equivalent of a small glass of wine, a measure of spirits, or half a pint of beer. When staying within your weekly allowance, try to have an alcohol-free night or two in order to give your liver a rest and time to recover itself.

Smoking

Although cigarettes are not a food, smoking is a subject that falls naturally under the heading of diet, especially since we may be reluctant to give up smoking for fear of putting on weight. Sadly, reluctance to give up cigarettes can have serious implications for our overall state of health, since smoking can be responsible for a staggeringly wide range of health problems including an increased risk of lung cancer, bronchitis, circulatory problems, heart disease, high blood pressure, osteoporosis, vitamin deficiency, digestive disorders and signs of premature ageing. The positive health benefits of giving up smoking are enormous, even if it does require great willpower, and single-mindedness. Also bear in mind that if we follow the general dietary advice in this chapter by eating plenty of fresh, unrefined foods, taking regular exercise and being wary of sugary snacks, giving up smoking need not necessarily result in our putting on unwanted pounds. Don't forget that some alternative therapies can also help wean us off addictions such as smoking:

possible help may be obtained from an acupuncturist, hypnotherapist, or homoeopath.

Salt

Although a small amount of salt is needed in the diet in order to maintain fluid balance in the body and discourage muscular cramps, an excess of salt can affect the delicate balance between potassium and sodium. Resulting problems can include a potassium deficiency, heart disease, or a tendency towards high blood pressure. Even if we avoid adding salt to our meals at the table, it is helpful to remember that if we eat a regular amount of convenience foods we are running the risk of eating a large amount of sodium along with additional food flavourings and artificial preservatives that are added during preparation. Bear in mind also that a taste for salt can become an addiction; in other words, the more we rely on salt to give food its flavour, the more salt we are likely to need in order to continue satisfying our taste buds.

The following points will help to put the advice given above into a practical, easily-applied context that we can use on a day-to-day basis in order to improve the overall quality of our diets. Do bear in mind that these are just general guidelines, not hard-and-fast rules graven in stone. Always remember that, in the end, it is up to you to use this information as creatively as you wish. This is absolutely essential if the advice in this chapter is to come alive for each of us: after all, we are all individuals with our own personal preferences, body rhythms and psychological motivation. As a result, what works brilliantly for one may be a disaster for another. Nowhere is this more true than with regard to our eating patterns, since a major reason why many of us abandon trying to improve the quality of our diet is our frustration at just not being able to find an eating plan that suits us.

Taking all this into consideration, the information given below sets out to inform, rather than make you feel guilty about all the things you may have done wrong up to now. Most important of all, using these general guidelines you should be able to enjoy the freedom and pleasure of a lively social life without feeling confused or guilty. This section assumes that you have no health problems such as diabetes, or allergic conditions such as coeliac disease, which require a special dietary approach. In other words, it is understood that those who take on board the following advice are in generally good health.

Above all, remember to be positive when using this advice. In other words, rather than longing for foods in the prohibited category, transform your eating habits positively by concentrating on the foods that can be eaten very freely. Then, instead of regarding eating well as a restrictive or frugal exercise, we can begin to see that many of the foods we love to eat can be part and parcel of a healthier way of eating.

Energising foods to concentrate on

- As many helpings of steamed or raw fresh fruit and vegetables as possible, either as a main meal in the form of a large mixed salad or as a side portion of mixed vegetables.
- Fish of all kinds, grilled, baked, steamed, or lightly stir-fried in a little olive oil. Avoid battered or deep-fried fish.
- Pasta.
- Brown rice, pulses and beans.
- Sauces made from tomatoes and fresh herbs as a quick and easy accompaniment for pasta, baked potatoes or brown rice.
- Home-made soups using fresh vegetables in season, or with additional bulk in winter and spring from beans and pulses.
- White meat such as chicken or turkey. Although buying free-range birds is preferable, bear in mind that the regulations only refer to the way that the birds are housed, not to the way they are fed. As a result, chemical foods and/or drugs may still be used. It is always best to buy organic where practical; failing this, ask questions about the food given to free-range birds.
- Salad dressing made from cold-pressed sunflower or safflower oil and vinegar, or yoghurt blended with herbs, instead of mayonnaise or salad cream.

- Semi-skimmed milk.
- Natural yoghurt. Avoid the low fat, low calorie varieties that make liberal use of artificial sweeteners. Opt instead for natural-flavoured bio yoghurt: this is delicious on its own, but if boredom sets in, brighten up the flavour by adding seasonal fresh fruit, cinnamon, or a small amount of honey.
- Filtered or mineral water. Drink regular amounts during the day, aiming for an optimum amount of five to six large glasses.
- Fresh fruit juices or cocktails that can be made on demand using a fruit juicer or blender.

'So-so' foods to eat in moderation

- If it is really hard to go without red meat, choose organically farmed produce and avoid eating meat on consecutive nights. In other words, if you have a meal including red meat, concentrate for the next few nights on eating fish, salads, or pulses and grains mixed together. On the other hand, if you are on holiday abroad for a couple of weeks and it is really difficult to avoid meat-based dishes on the menu, don't panic. Enjoy the food while you are there and make sure when you return home that you avoid red meat for a few weeks.
- Butter.
- Cheeses such as Edam, Gouda, Brie, Camembert, fromage frais, or some ewe's or goat's cheese.
- Eggs (boiled, poached, or scrambled, but not fried).
- Puddings: have a minimum of three or four nights a week when you choose fresh fruit or yoghurt instead: you'll be amazed at how quickly sweet desserts lose their appeal and taste far too rich once you have fewer of them.
- Alcohol: opt for a glass of dry white or red wine in preference to regular consumption of spirits with sweetened mixers.
- Crème fraiche.
- Coffee or tea.
- Biscuits or cakes.

'No-no' foods to be avoided

- Heavily processed foods that have been dehydrated.
- Any foods that have large amounts of salt added to them. Also remember to avoid cooking with salt or adding it to dishes before eating. The best plan usually is not to have a salt grinder or cellar on the table.
- Items that have a large fat content such as salami, smoked meat, sausages, or pâté. These foods also have the added drawback that they often include a hefty proportion of additives.
- Foods made from white flour and sugar.
- Fizzy drinks containing a large amount of 'hidden' sugar.
- Any items that have been exposed to a range of chemical processes or genetic modification, or that have artificial sweeteners or flavourings added to them in order to make them more palatable.
- Potato crisps or other snack foods.
- Any items saturated in fat such as garlic bread, unless the latter is made with olive oil as a very occasional treat.
- Cream.
- Chinese or Indian dishes in take-away form, or as commercially-prepared dishes. Delicious as these can be, they do unfortunately include very large amounts of saturated fat (in Indian dishes), and chemical additives (in Chinese dishes). Instead, try stir-fried dishes that can be prepared at home using fresh vegetables, small amounts of seafood, fish or poultry, seasonings and virgin, cold-pressed olive oil.

Practical issues: cooking methods

When talking about improving the quality of our daily eating, there is little point in discussing the individual items involved if we forget to pay attention to the methods of cooking we use to make the foods enjoyable. In other words, we can take the healthiest and most energy-giving ingredients, but if we compromise on how we cook these items, we will not be getting the most out of what we eat. On the contrary, by using unhealthy methods of cooking, we could be turning foods that are good for us into foods that we need to avoid!

To use a practical example: potatoes are an excellent source of carbohydrate when they are baked, and become additionally nutritious if we also eat the skins. On the other hand, if we take the same ingredient and turn it into chipped potatoes, we have transformed it into a health hazard because of the amount of fat absorbed by the potatoes in the cooking process. The same effect would be created by making mashed potato using butter, margarine, lots of salt, or full-fat milk. On the other hand, if mashed potato is a favourite, reduce the potential high-fat and sodium problems by using low-fat milk, a little natural yoghurt, and pepper or nutmeg for seasoning.

When shopping, it also helps to pay attention to where we buy our ingredients if we want to get the maximum positive benefit from what we eat. For example, when you buy potatoes, look for organic varieties (these are increasingly easily available from major supermarket chains). It is worth making this effort because the storage chemicals can be absorbed as much as a quarter of an inch beneath the skin. If non-organic potatoes are boiled in their skins (in an attempt to preserve the nutrients that are stored just beneath the skin), there is a strong possibility that these chemicals will be driven further into the flesh of the vegetable while it is being cooked.

Also watch out for fruit or vegetables with skins that look or feel waxy, or just too perfect; this can be an indication of chemical residue left on the skin. In contrast, organically grown fruit and vegetables may look less obviously attractive and more flawed, but they have the advantage of being cultivated without the use of chemical pesticides and fertilisers. As a result, they are likely to be of greater overall nutritional value than the superficially flawless varieties sold in shrink-wrap packages in supermarkets.

The advice given below provides a broad overview of the basic cooking methods that preserve the maximum nutritional status of the foods we eat, and the other methods that may result in a hefty loss of essential nutrients such as vitamins and minerals.

Optimum cooking methods

Steaming

This is definitely the preferred way of cooking vegetables, because a higher proportion of essential vitamins and minerals are preserved than when the same items are boiled. It also has the additional advantage that vegetables remain crisp and fresher-tasting after they have been steamed, unlike boiled vegetables which can turn into something notoriously soggy and tasteless. Don't forget that steaming can also be used as a method of cooking fish that has a delicate taste and texture.

Stir-frying

This is an excellent method of cooking a whole range of ingredients, including poultry, fish, shellfish, or vegetables, without adding a large amount of fat or losing the texture and flavour of fresh ingredients. It is also a very practical way of cooking for those of us who want a quick, imaginative and easy way of preparing our food. When stir-frying, always use a monounsaturated oil such as cold-pressed olive oil rather than solid margarine or animal fats such as butter.

Poaching

A clever way of lightly cooking fish without using extra fat, making sure that seasoned water is used rather than full-fat milk. Seasoning can be obtained from herbs and spices rather than adding lots of salt. Also an excellent alternative way of cooking eggs.

Raw foods

Don't forget that fruit and vegetables are best eaten raw whenever possible, since essential vitamins can be lost in cooking. Vitamin C can also be lost through oxidation into the atmosphere if raw foods are chopped and prepared a few hours in advance of eating. Also remember to scrub vegetable and fruit skins thoroughly if they may have come from a dubious source.

Shallow frying or browning

This can be done with no oil, or with a small amount of cold-pressed olive oil for those foods that are too dry to exude their own moisture. Use a heavy pan over a steady heat and avoid washing pans in detergent in order to avoid sticking.

Grilling

Ideally, grill on a rack or griddle that allows fat to drain away during the cooking process. Avoid brushing additional fat on to food before grilling.

Roasting

Always the preferred way of cooking meat, since other methods such as frying involve the use of extra fat.

Fondue cookery

Avoid the hot oil method and use stock instead. Many fondue recipes suggest ways of using the fondue method to cook fish, shellfish, meat and poultry without oil.

Cooking methods to be avoided

Adding creamy sauces

Always make a point of avoiding recipes and dishes on menus which involve the addition of rich sauces, as these invariably include large helpings of cream and butter. When choosing a sauce as an accompaniment, always opt for a light, tomato-based sauce that can be spiced-up with garlic and herbs, or try a purée of brightly-coloured vegetables such as red peppers. Not only does this taste delicious, but it also provides us with a healthy source of anti-oxidant nutrients.

Deep-frying

Always to be avoided because this method of cooking adds a very high proportion of fat to any food, but especially to those items that absorb fat like a sponge (mushrooms or aubergines). This adds immediately to its calorific value and increases the possibility of the health risks associated with too high a consumption of dietary fat.

(See the section on free radicals in Chapter Two, p. 45).

Adding salt during cooking

Always avoid the temptation to add salt to food during the cooking process, use other herbs at the table instead. Never add bicarbonate of soda to vegetables in order to preserve their colour, since steaming is a healthier alternative that helps keep our greens green!

Boiling

Not the best way to cook vegetables because too high a proportion of vitamins and minerals leach into the liquid during the cooking process. Unfortunately, boiled vegetables also tend to be a disaster because they quickly pass from a crisp, appetising state to something limp, tasteless and colourless. On the other hand, if vegetables have been boiled, keep the cooking water to add to soups and sauces. There are also some ingredients that must be boiled, such as dried beans and pulses which have to be boiled in plenty of unsalted water until they are fully cooked. This is especially the case when preparing red kidney beans, which can be toxic if eaten partially cooked.

Microwaving

Although microwaving vegetables helps preserve their colour, crispness and a large proportion of their vitamin content, we should avoid relying too often on microwaving as a method of cooking. We do not yet have any clear picture of what long-term effects eating microwaved food may have on the body, and we still do not know what molecular changes may be happening to the food being cooked. The radiation emitted by microwave ovens also raises concerns of its own, so always make a point of never standing close to the oven while cooking is going on, and leave the food to stand for a minute or so after cooking is over.

'Trouble-shooting' strategies

This is the section where we find out the answers to some tricky but common questions about nutrition and discover how to rectify dietary imbalances which may occur at phases of our life when we are pressed for time and have to make do with a less than perfect approach to nutrition. Don't rely too heavily on these hints as a way of cutting nutritional corners on a permanent basis; they give practical advice on how to prevent a time of nutritional compromise from turning into a nutritional nightmare. It is also important to realise that if we have information on straightforward steps we can take to get things back on track quickly, we are less likely to go completely off the rails thinking that we might as well be hanged for a nutritional sheep as a lamb!

Problem 1: Too many convenience foods for too long

If there are frequent periods of time when we rely almost exclusively on ready meals, due perhaps to a demanding job with long or irregular hours, we need to ensure that we follow some basic rules as a nutritional damage limitation exercise. Always try to buy meals that are as close to their natural state as possible: in other words steer clear of anything that is dehydrated, freeze dried and full of artificial additives, colourings and preservatives. Aim instead for fish or chicken dishes that involve no more than light grilling and adding a pre-prepared fresh sauce. Avoid convenience foods that have a mind-bogglingly remote sell-by date, and try to avoid too many items that are salted, preserved, smoked or charred (reasons for this are given above in the general list of foods to avoid on a regular basis). When heating ready-prepared dishes, avoid microwaving them in the plastic container in which they have been sold; transfer them instead to a glass or ceramic bowl before putting in the microwave. Although it takes a little longer, this is worth doing in order to avoid changes taking place during the microwaving process which involve the leaching of oestrogen-type chemicals from the plastic container into the food. Include a helping of fresh vegetables or mixed salad, and finish off with fresh fruit rather than a pudding.

Problem 2 : Increased alcohol intake

First of all, be honest about evaluating just how much you are drinking in a week. The best way of doing this is to establish how many units a week you are having; a unit is a small glass of wine, a pub measure of spirits, or half a pint of beer or lager. If your amount is around fourteen units or more and you are a woman, or if it is around twenty-one units or more and you are a man, it's time to do something about it. When we are stressed there is every chance that as well as having too high an intake of alcohol, we shall also be smoking too much and eating irregularly and not very well. If this sounds familiar, a course of a good-quality multivitamin and multi-mineral supplement can do a great deal to get us back on track by supplying us with the vitamins and minerals depleted by drinking and smoking. It may also be helpful to take an extra daily dose of 500 mgs of vitamin C if you have been catching one minor infection after another since being stressed. At the same time, give yourself a couple of weeks where you have a break from alcohol altogether, choosing palatable alternatives such as sparkling mineral water with a twist of lime or lemon, fruit-flavoured sparkling drinks, or one of the increasingly imaginative herbal sparkling drinks which provide an excellent alternative to wine at dinner or parties. It's also possible to order non-alcoholic cocktails at bars; these look and taste much the same as the alcoholic variety, but without the drawbacks. When returning to drinking alcohol, establish a pattern of always staying well below the recommended unit allowance and having three or four evenings a week when alcohol is avoided in order to give your liver a chance to recharge and regenerate itself.

Problem 3: The merits and demerits of eating butter or alternative fats

However complicated the arguments might seem which surround the issue of eating butter versus synthetic fats, the reality is much simpler than it might seem at first. Basically, we should be cutting down *whatever* fat we need so that it makes up no more than 20 per cent of our daily dietary intake. However harsh this may sound, it is the only sensible course to take, since each source of fat available has its own associated health problems. On the other hand, when we keep the amount of fat in our diet healthily low, regardless of the source it comes from, we appear to reduce our risk of developing heart and circulatory problems, or cancer of the breast and colon. We should also find that reduction of our overall fat intake brings the welcome benefit of helping us reach a healthy weight, since dietary fats are one of the most concentrated sources of calories available to us. We have an even greater chance of benefiting from losing excess weight and improving our overall nutritional status if we reduce our intake of fat and refined sugar at the same time.

If we want to look after our circulatory systems we should avoid eating regular or generous amounts of any of the following saturated fats: hard cheeses, full-fat milk and soft cheeses, red meat (beef, pork, and bacon), chocolate and butter. On the other hand, some vegetable oils (such as margarine that is solid at room temperature) can also bring their own problems; as a result, they should be used very sparingly in the diet. Possible problems associated with poly-unsaturated fats heated to very high temperatures include the presence of free radicals. These are very unstable molecules which appear to be implicated in a host of potential health problems including circulatory problems and some cancers. This is why we should never use hydrogenated vegetable fats that are solid at room temperature for frying.

For more information on the problems associated with free radicals and the use of anti-oxidant nutrients as a way of combating their harmful effects, see p. 45. Heating commercially-prepared oils

damages the beneficial essential fatty acids present in polyunsaturated oils. Further tampering with refined oils, by using solvents
to achieve a lighter colour and greater clarity of appearance, can
cause additional problems through the removal of more essential
fatty acids, trace vitamins and minerals and antioxidant nutrients.

Hydrogenated vegetable fats that are solid at room temperature
have additional problems in the form of trans fatty acids, which are
produced when the oil is heated to a high temperature and hydrogen
is passed through it. The trans fatty acids created as a result of this
process resemble the structure of saturated fats and may give rise to
the same health hazards when eaten regularly and in generous
amounts.

So, we might ask, what do we do in order to minimise the health
risks associated with eating fats? The answer has already been given
above: eat any form of fat in strict moderation and use small amounts
of butter in preference to hydrogenated margarine. When cooking,
choose virgin, cold-pressed olive oil, which appears to play a positive
role in protecting the heart and circulatory system. Other oils that
have been hailed as giving us extra protection against heart disease
include fish oils, which are rich in omega 3 fatty acids.

Problem 4: The basic arguments for and against being a vegetarian

Thank goodness the days are long gone when vegetarianism conjured
up images of style-suicide, including tasteless nut cutlets and socks
worn with open-toed sandals and shorts! These days, vegetarianism,
like ecology, is perceived as a pressing issue that is extremely relevant
to the world we live in today and want our children to rejoice in
tomorrow. With the BSE and salmonella scares of the recent past,
the real problems associated with meat and poultry farming and the
manufacture and storage of dairy products have become front page
news. If we also consider the growing concern about the use of
antibiotics and steroids to stimulate unnatural growth in animals
destined for slaughter, the picture gets even more alarming and grim.

Other questions about the advisability of eating meat concern the role that red meat can play in raising our blood cholesterol levels, as well as the tendency of red meat to ferment and putrefy in the gut during the extended process needed to break down the nutrients into a form that can be utilised by the body. These two factors have led to the suggestion that a very regular or high consumption of red meat may be implicated in the rise of two of the killer diseases of our time: coronary heart disease and cancer.

One of the arguments against adopting vegetarianism is that so much planning and careful thought is needed to work out where the essential protein in our diets will come from. However, this objection is often made into a much greater obstacle than it need be in reality. Provided we combine beans and pulses with grains at one serving, we are sure of getting a complete protein. It really is quite simple: if we consider the three food groups of pulses, cereals and nuts, all we have to do is combine any two of these and we have a biologically complete protein. It is generally true to say that concern about the risk of vegetarians lacking protein in their diet is exaggerated; with a basic knowledge of nutrition it is really very easy to ensure that more than adequate sources of protein are provided. Problems are only likely to occur where adopting a vegetarian way of eating is interpreted as omitting meat and fish from each meal within the context of an already careless or poor-quality diet.

However, it is important for vegetarians to be aware that mass-market vegetables also run the risk of being contaminated through the use of pesticides. They should also take into account the issue of genetically modified ingredients, discussed below. The pesticide problem can be overcome by making a point of buying organic produce; otherwise, always make sure that vegetable and fruit skins are peeled or scrubbed thoroughly before preparing and eating.

If we look at the practicalities of the situation in a ruthlessly pragmatic way, there are a number of reasons why becoming a strict vegetarian may be very difficult for many of us. Some of us may have a professional and personal lifestyle that makes the restrictions very difficult, especially if our job involves regular travelling to countries where vegetarianism is not the norm. Others may feel that, much as they may sympathise with many of the moral arguments put forward by vegetarians, they just do not have the necessary resolve and commitment to give up fish or meat dishes. Being a strict vegan (which involves excluding all animal items from the diet including dairy products and eggs) presents us with an even greater challenge which may be out of the question for many of us.

The following practical suggestions are intended as guidance for those who may be concerned about the risks of eating meat, but also feel that they are not in a position to become a committed vegetarian. These are basic steps that can be taken to improve the overall quality of anyone's diet on a regular basis.

- Try to locate sources of organically farmed red meat or, if these are difficult to find, look for 'conservation grade' meat farmed in a conventional way, but without medicines being given to animals on a routine, herd basis.
- Make a point of not eating red meat several days in a row: by having long gaps in between meat eating, our digestive systems are given a greater chance of recovering.
- Choose free-range chicken or fish where possible. Remember that the protein found in fish and chicken is more readily accessible and more easily digested than the protein in red meat. When buying fish, avoid farmed trout or salmon, because these are exposed to chemicals and fungicides and experience living conditions as crowded as those suffered by battery hens.
- Even if finding organically grown vegetables seems difficult, make sure that you have a minimum of four to six servings of fruit or vegetables every day. After all, it's better to have fruit and vegetables from a non-organic source than none at all. Fresh fruit juice can count as one portion, and if it has been freshly squeezed it will provide the maximum proportion of nutrients. For more specific advice on fruit juice and vitamin C content, see the section on vitamin C in Chapter Two ('Immune System Boosters'), p. 47.
- Perhaps most important of all, remember that variety is an essential part of healthy eating. This is every bit as true for vegetarians as it is for those of us who eat meat and fish. Relying on a diet of chips, beans and white bread is not very likely to be

much of an improvement on a regular intake of hamburgers and milkshakes. In other words, just cutting out the animal products doesn't of itself guarantee improved nutritional status! On the other hand, the variety in texture, colour and flavour to be found in whole grains, pulses, raw vegetables and fruit in season should make eating vegetarian dishes a delicious experience that is also delightful to the eye.

Bear in mind that substituting large or regular quantities of cheese for meat isn't necessarily a healthy step forward in our eating patterns. Hard cheeses tend to be one of the most generous sources of saturated fat and should be eaten in moderation by anyone concerned about their overall intake of dietary fat.

In addition, we should make a point of adopting as flexible an attitude as possible towards what we eat. After all, we don't eat just to provide our bodies with fuel: we are also satisfying a fundamentally important sensual appetite. Eating should also often be a shared pleasure, where we experience the conviviality and warmth of sharing with others. If we lose this basic aspect of the pleasure of eating, by adopting a diet that is too rigid and uncompromising, we run the risk of losing an essential part of our lives; loss of pleasure and a sense of deprivation should not play any part in a holistic experience of living. Above all, remember that, however you choose to eat, feeling relaxed is one of the most important aids to a healthy digestion. On the other hand, feeling guilty or tense is one of the greatest obstacles we can present to a smooth digestive process.

Problem 5: Vitamin supplements

Advice on the vexed question of whether we need to take vitamin and mineral supplements or not tends to vary from those who insist that nutritional supplements *must* be taken, even when our diets include the most varied, healthy and fresh ingredients, to those who claim that the whole trend towards taking supplements is no more than an expensive and unnecessary fad. Surely all we need to do is enjoy a basic diet and our nutritional needs will be easily met?

As in so many situations, the answer probably lies somewhere
the middle of these two opposing views. For example, those of
who have a history of erratic eating patterns or eating disorders a
almost certainly going to be deficient in basic nutrients, whi
smokers, drinkers, or women who take the contraceptive pill w
also be robbing their bodies of essential vitamins such as C and
complex. Regular exposure to the toxins found in cigarettes, atmo
pheric pollution, or alcohol can leave us open to a variety of serio
health risks, including the development of degenerative diseas
Specific nutrients called anti-oxidants (vitamin A, beta-caroten
vitamin C, vitamin E and selenium) are thought to be helpful
countering some of the detrimental effects of toxicity. For mo
information on the use of anti-oxidant supplements, see p. 45.

Additional situations where supplements can play an invaluab
role include:

- A protracted history of emotional and physical stress
- A tendency to recurrent infections, colds, flu, or chest infectior
- Long-term use of conventional drugs such as steroids
- Careless eating habits in the past, including a tendency to rely c
  'fast foods' and eat very few fresh vegetables and fruit
- A history of over-commitment to exercise with a tendency
  easy injury
- Approaching the menopause.

However, it is also very important to rectify dietary deficiencie
rather than rely totally on supplements as a fast-fix for our problem
Any benefits from appropriate supplementation are likely to t
enhanced by a diet that includes a generous proportion of fresl
raw foods, protein, complex carbohydrates from whole grains ar
starches and a small quantity of fat such as virgin, cold-pressed oliv
oil.

It is generally not advisable to try to diagnose nutritional de
ficiencies for ourselves, and it can be especially harmful to begi
taking mega-doses of individual nutrients which, taken inappropr
ately, can actually set off an imbalance. If a deficiency looks possibl

nsult a specialist in nutritional medicine who will be able to assess
ur individual nutritional state and suggest an appropriate course
action.

When we are talking about the possibility of taking a toxic dose
vitamin supplements, it is crucially important to distinguish
tween the two distinct types of vitamins: those that are water
luble and those that are fat soluble. Fat-soluble vitamins can be
ored by the body, with the risk that any significant excess will not
eliminated by the body but stored in the tissues, leading to a
otential toxic build-up. The vitamins that fall into this category
clude vitamins A, D, E and K. This problem of a potentially toxic
uild-up is one of the reasons why making an effort to obtain our
sic nutrients from a high-quality diet is preferable to relying too
uch on supplements. It is possible to eat enormous amounts of
rrots and carrot juice and eventually reach a state of toxic overload,
ut this would take a great deal of single-mindedness and effort. On
e other hand, it would be much easier to exceed the recommended
take of vitamin A by taking an excessive amount of capsules or
blets.

Water-soluble vitamins, on the other hand, are flushed out of the
ody in the urine and stools, so a toxic reaction to less than mega-
osage is not likely to be a problem. These include vitamins C and
complex. The most common sign of ingesting an excessive amount
these vitamins will probably be a bad bout of diarrhoea and acidity
the stomach (except for the example of B6 given below). However,
so take care not to use mega-doses of vitamin C routinely which
n have the adverse effect of depleting minerals from our bodies.

We should also be cautious with mega-doses of Vitamin E. This
tamin has a reputation for being of general benefit to the circulatory
stem, as well as for its anti-oxidant properties. However, it can
ave an adverse effect when taken in mega-doses on those who suffer
om high blood pressure if a large dose is taken abruptly. It is better
build dosage up slowly. Vitamin B6, although water-soluble, has
een shown to set off neurological problems when given in mega-
oses in isolation from the other vitamins that make up the B
omplex group.

If we feel that we could do with a general, all-purpose nutrition
supplement after a period of stress, it can be helpful to take a cour
of a good-quality combined vitamin and mineral supplement. Th
following suggestions are general guidelines for a suitably conse
vative dosage. However, if you are in any doubt or feel that yo
needs are more specialised, consult a practitioner in nutrition
medicine rather than experiment on your own.

Vitamin A 5000 ius
Beta-carotene 5000 ius
Vitamin B1 25–50 mg
Vitamin B2 25–50 mg
Vitamin B3 25–75 mg
Vitamin B6 10–100 mg
Vitamin B12 10–40 mcg
Folic acid 200 mcg
Biotin 100 mcg
Vitamin C 1000 mg
Vitamin E 100–300 ius
Calcium 100–300 mg
Magnesium 50-150 mg
Iron 10 mg
Zinc 10–15 mg
Manganese 5 mg
Selenium 100 mcg
Chromium 25–50 mcg

Problem 6: Genetically modified foods

Although this is still a relatively recent phenomenon, seriou
questions have already been raised regarding the safety of foo
containing genetically modified ingredients such as soya beans, maiz
or tomatoes. One of the main concerns about genetically modifie
ingredients is that they may have undergone significant chemic
changes and we don't yet know what effects these changes may hav
on our bodies.

While GM foods are such an unknown quantity, it would seem to make very good sense to avoid them as far as possible. However, this may be a little more difficult than it seems at first glance. According to Patrick Holford, as many as half the products sold on supermarket shelves are the product of some variety of genetic engineering, with the result that we may be unwittingly eating GM foods on a regular basis. The range of foods that may contain genetically modified ingredients is very wide, and may include convenience foods, soft drinks, biscuits, bread, chocolate and baby foods. In order to limit exposure to GM products, always check the list of ingredients in each item you buy, paying particular attention to those that contain soya, maize, or tomatoes. As always, the safest option is to choose organic produce wherever possible, either from supermarkets that stock organic lines or from health food stores.

4

Exercise Boosters

Our bodies are designed to be used and stretched if they are to be kept in peak condition. In the same way that a car will rust and lose its mechanical smoothness if it is left unused for long periods of time, our bodies will grow stiff, inflexible, and prone to weakness when they are left to become increasingly immobile. Apart from the physical benefit that fitness brings, we also experience improved emotional resilience, reduction in stress-related symptoms, greater resistance to infection, and boosted self-confidence and self-esteem when we engage in regular exercise. Isn't it strange, when we consider the benefits involved, that so many of us have a mental block when it comes to getting fit?

However, for many of us, just thinking of the word exercise may make us wish that the whole craze for physical fitness would go away. We are constantly confronted by images of super-fit and super-toned bodies that often make us feel lost causes. The problems can be greater for women or men who are painfully self-conscious; the knowledge that we have areas of our bodies that we would really prefer to keep under cover (due to lack of muscle tone or the ever-present cellulite) can make us feel very inhibited about baring our bodies in the swimming pool or the gym.

However, the secret of discovering the magic of physical fitness is much nearer our grasp than we might imagine: the trick is to shed our preconceptions of outmoded and outdated systems of exercise. At the outset, we have to move beyond the idea that fulfilling our physical potential involves suffering; nothing could be further from the truth. To benefit fully from any form of exercise, we must enjoy the sheer physicality and sensuous pleasure that comes from stretching and moving our bodies.

Once we have found the optimum combination of exercise for ourselves, we can in many ways begin to live in true harmony with ourselves. This is a wonderful discovery because many of us who feel unfit may have the distinct sensation that we are at odds with our bodies. This is connected with having an idealised image of how we want to be, only to find it dashed as soon as we catch sight of ourselves in a mirror. If this goes on for long enough, the impact on our self-confidence can be very destructive, compromising our ability to feel contented with our bodies and the way they look and perform.

A new model of fitness

Without being conscious of it, many of us were alienated by the image of physical fitness presented to us during the eighties. 'Going for the burn', combined with the 'no pain, no gain' approach, was enough to put anyone off who didn't respond to a tough approach to fitness.

Unfortunately, this competitive and uncompromising atmosphere in the gym led many of us to push our bodies beyond their optimum limits, with the result that too many needless injuries occurred. Back pain from unsupported forward bends, combined with joint injuries in the knee and ankle as a result of jogging for too long on a hard surface, put many of us off the idea of physical fitness eighties-style.

There was the added problem that aerobics classes were far too large and too fast to allow special attention to be given to beginners. As a result, too many people jumped in at the deep end and floundered.

Although the way that the general concepts of physical fitness and the importance of exercise came to the forefront in the eighties was basically good, it was, unfortunately, a rather unbalanced perspective, with the maximum emphasis being placed on achieving the perfect body shape. Sadly, other considerations were too often ignored or sacrificed in pursuit of this elusive goal.

However, the fresh model of all-round fitness that has emerged during the nineties emphasises the essential need for physical, mental and emotional balance. Within this general context, the ideal form of exercise is one that helps us achieve maximum well-being of mind and body. This marks a strong departure from the excesses of the eighties; the current ideal form of physical movement encourages us to work in harmony with our fitness potential and develop a heightened sense of what positively challenges our bodies. This is quite a different process to punishing our bodies by repeating mindless repetitive movements in the hope that we can transform our physical appearance.

Integrated exercise

It is noticeable that those who most enjoy being physically fit have succeeded in making exercise a seamless part of their daily routine. They have moved beyond seeing physical activity as something separate that requires investing in specialised fitness clothes and an expensive subscription to a gym. As a result, instead of regarding exercise as a chore, we can get fit far more successfully by doing things we enjoy.

Once we begin to enjoy exercise from this integrated perspective, we can begin to approach the whole issue of physical fitness from a fresh angle. Most significantly of all, we shall probably find that, as our perception of fitness evolves and changes, we shall begin slowly to see ourselves transformed from couch potatoes into strong, resilient and confident individuals who take pleasure in what our bodies can do as our fitness levels improve.

Don't be put off by thinking that this has to happen all at once and that it is fine for others, but just not your sort of thing. The changes described above take place by making small, cumulative adjustments. All we have to do is identify enjoyable activities that we can incorporate into our lives which will lead us towards increased and balanced body awareness.

Freedom of choice

When we put our minds to it, the potential range of choice open to us is encouragingly wide, so that all of us should be able to find ways of getting fit that will suit us as individuals. The question of meeting our individual needs is of paramount importance, whether it is finding a suitable system of physical fitness that suits our temperament, or a form of alternative medical treatment that treats us as an individual with our own unique mental, emotional and physical identity.

We live in exciting times for personal growth, because a fundamental change appears to be taking place. Many of us are waking up to the fact that what is perfectly appropriate for one person is not remotely suitable for another. This can be applied right across the board to embrace choices in health care, dietary preferences, social life, career goals, or general lifestyle.

This need to fulfil our individual demands is also reflected in the forms of exercise we ultimately choose. Many of us are not in the least bit interested in running marathons, high-impact aerobics classes, or heavy-duty body building. On the other hand, this doesn't mean that we can't have fun swimming, playing tennis, badminton or volleyball, skiing, rebounding, aqua aerobics, or just plain and simple walking.

Remember that we can all develop by making the smallest of

changes. They may seem very minor at the time, but they establish our intention to change by engaging us in what may seem a tiny commitment. Let's say that we want to start doing aqua aerobics because we love contact with water, but hitherto the whole physical fitness phenomenon has passed us by because we felt intimidated by it. We can begin to experience working with the resistance of water at home by doing some simple exercises in our baths. This has the double advantage of getting us started in the privacy of our homes while also getting us used to moving muscles that we probably didn't know we had.

It's also extremely important always to choose a form of exercise that we positively enjoy; it is so much easier to continue our commitment if we are engaged in something that we look forward to doing. There is little point in choosing a form of fitness activity that bores the pants off us, since human nature dictates that we will give this up at the earliest opportunity – and who could blame us?

To get started, it's just a question of using our imaginations and looking beyond the forms of exercise we may have rejected before as being unappealing or downright unsuitable.

Fringe benefits

If we continue to look at the positive, discovering the fun of playing sport as an adult can bring a host of surprising pleasures. This is an especially delightful bonus for those of us who were put off by the spartan way that so many sporting activities were taught at school. Many unfit adults have probably been put off sport or physical fitness classes for good by haunting memories of freezing on a sports pitch on a grey winter's day, just wishing they could be somewhere else.

On the other hand, if this sounds familiar to you, do give a fun sounding sport a second try as an adult, especially if you have the encouragement and support of enough of your friends. The chances are that you will be amazed at how the sheer enjoyment of playing port with friends can give an enormous boost to your social life. In addition, the activity will boost your overall vitality and increase our self-esteem and self-confidence.

Follow the impulses of your mood and you can tailor your fitness activities to suit your frame of mind. There will be days when you feel like having some space to yourself and prefer to relax and unwind with some stretching exercises or yoga postures at home. On a more outgoing and up-beat day, you may want nothing more than to go swimming or walking with a group of friends. This brings us back to the fundamental importance of recognising and satisfying our individual needs. The ultimate trick is to make our fitness programme as fluid as possible in order to allow for our fluctuations of mood. This approach will always lead to success, because it avoids a strait-jacketed, regimented approach to exercise that does not allow for spontaneity or joy.

General health benefits

Exercise and the immune system

There are a host of health benefits associated with regular, rhythmic exercise. One of the most important is the conditioning of the immune system. The fundamental value of this becomes clear when we recognise how dependent we are on our immune systems to protect us against infection and disease.

If our immune systems are to work at peak efficiency, we must have a healthy lymphatic system. The latter includes the lymph nodes found in the neck, armpits and groin. When our immune systems are working as they should, toxins and dead cells are transported via the lymphatic fluid contained in the lymphatic vessels to the lymph nodes. It is the function of the lymph nodes to filter out any impurities before the lymphatic fluid is channelled back to the bloodstream.

Unlike the circulatory system, which has the benefit of the

powerful pumping action of the heart to propel the blood aroun
the body, the lymphatic system is dependent on a quite differer
mechanism to keep lymphatic fluid moving. For the essential proces
of detoxification to take place, the lymphatic system depends on th
muscle pressure that occurs as the body moves, or on the sheer forc
of gravity.

Given this dependence of the lymphatic system on muscula
activity, we can see how regular exercise can play a particularl
important role. By engaging in frequent physical effort we ar
effectively supporting and stimulating the nourishing, water
balancing and eliminative functions of the lymphatic system. If w
take into account the centrally important role played by the lymph
atic system (including the lymph nodes) in antibody production, w
are clearly supporting our body's defence mechanism if we exercis
regularly.

In addition, improving the movement of lymphatic fluid is als
an invaluable way of helping eliminate the cellulite that can be a
unwelcome feature of the skin on thighs, buttocks and hips.

Exercise and stress

Many of us already know that regular exercise is an excellent way o
reducing stress. During extended periods of stressful activity we ar
likely to overproduce adrenalin which has the knock-on effect o
making our blood sugar levels unstable. This situation is too ofte
aggravated by reaching for the 'quick-fix' foods that attract us whe
the pace gets too much for us. These items include salt, sugar, alcoho
strong coffee and tea, which will give us an initial boost by raisin
blood sugar levels, but are all too quickly followed by a furthe
plummeting of energy as the pancreas secretes insulin in an attemp
to bring blood sugar levels down. If this process goes on for lon
enough, we develop unstable blood sugar levels that swing regularl
from one extreme to another, and often result in feeling exhauste
dizzy, jittery and generally unwell.

If the stress and 'quick-fix solution' continues, a downward spir
is inevitable and leaves us with increasingly depleted energy level

However, the good news is that this downward spiral can be broken by using exercise to disrupt a chronic stress pattern. This is especially relevant to those of us who have high-powered and sedentary jobs, because we are especially at risk of building up accumulated stress during the day.

Regular exercise provides an excellent channel for burning off excess adrenalin while increasing the blood supply that transports oxygen and nutrients to each cell in the body. As a result, appropriate exercise can either tranquillise or energise, depending on our individual needs and our combination of exercises. As our bodies begin to work more efficiently more energy is conserved, with the bonus that we will feel fitter than we thought possible.

Exercise and emotional balance

We may feel that exercise gives us a sense of increased well-being as a direct result of our bodies becoming leaner, slender, and stronger. There is also the undeniable sensation of pleasure that comes from inhabiting a body that moves with ease and flexibility, especially if we experience the sense of freedom that comes with running. However, beyond all these important features, a chemical change also occurs when we engage in regular aerobic exercise that promotes a sense of well-being.

Chemicals called endorphins, which produce pleasure-giving sensations, are secreted into the bloodstream. Endorphins are also naturally-occurring anti-depressants with a sedative, calming effect which produces the 'high' that follows aerobic activity. This is why anyone who is diagnosed as suffering from mild depression or anxiety is likely to benefit from engaging in regular physical exercise. It has been suggested by the Exercise Laboratory of California that taking a brisk walk may be at least as effective as taking a 400 mg dose of a tranquilliser.

Using regular exercise to reduce feelings of anxiety or depression also has definite advantages over relying on a chemical drug to contain our symptoms. Engaging in enjoyable physical movement brings additional benefits such as healthier heart and lung function, as well as the improved performance of the immune system outlined above. Although sometimes necessary in severe cases of anxiety and depression, the use of anti-depressants and tranquillisers brings none of these advantages and often has side-effects that can reduce our overall experience of health and vitality.

Exercise and heart health

It is easy to overlook the fact that our hearts are made of muscle, and if the muscle tissue in our legs, arms and backs needs to be kept in prime condition in order to function at peak capacity, the same is true of our hearts. The greatest difference, of course, is that we are able to see if the muscles in our upper arms or thighs are beginning to show signs of getting flabby and out of condition, and this often prompts us to do something about the situation before the degeneration goes too far. When it comes to the condition of our hearts, on the other hand, there are not likely to be obvious signs of a problem until things have progressed to a potentially serious stage. At this point we may experience problems with breathlessness or pains in the chest on exertion.

However, if we take action earlier rather than later, it is possible to improve the condition of our hearts so that they work more efficiently. In order to support our cardiovascular performance (the functioning of our hearts and circulatory systems), we must exercise our heart muscles. This needs to be done through regular aerobic activity which makes our hearts pump harder in order to supply the other muscles of the body with fresh blood that is rich in oxygen. (See below for a list of activities that fall into the aerobic category.)

The benefits of appropriate physical exercise include making our heart muscles larger and more efficient and lowering our resting pulse rate (generally regarded as an indicator of a healthy and well-functioning heart). This happens because as the heart becomes bigger, it is able to pump a greater volume of blood with each beat, with the result that it is not required to beat as frequently to achieve the same result. Once you gain in fitness, your pulse should get slower and you should find that it returns more rapidly to normal after physical exertion.

Although even moderate physical activity is better than nothing at all, we should be aiming towards half an hour of aerobic exercise four or five times a week. Don't panic and think that this has to be done from the start, because it would be foolish to jump in at the deep end and positively unwise if we are starting from scratch. Start sensibly, with five minutes of heart-conditioning exercise every other day, and add on an extra five minutes each week. We need to be sensitive about working within our physical capabilities and only going further when we feel it is comfortably within our range. If we feel that we need to stay with five minutes every other day for three weeks before we are ready to make that extra effort, that's fine, provided we get there in the end.

Basic breathing

Before embarking on any exercise regime, it is worth spending some time considering the basic importance of good breathing technique. Without correct breathing we cannot get the maximum benefit from whatever form of exercise we do.

Many of us overlook how well we breathe because it is an involuntary function. In other words, because it can happen without our conscious control, we pay less attention to it than we should, often because our minds are occupied elsewhere. On the other hand, by learning some very straightforward breathing techniques we become aware of how it feels to be in tune with our bodies.

Enhanced flexibility

When we concentrate on the way we breathe while we are engaged in exercise, we discover that dizziness and light-headedness cease to be a problem. In addition, breathing correctly while stretching can do a great deal to increase flexibility. This is partly why certain forms of exercise such as Yoga embrace a central concept of breath control and regulation as a way of maximising stretching capacity, deepening relaxation and calming the mind.

Enhanced oxygen absorption

The more we engage in physical exercise the more we need to become aware of our breathing in order to gain the maximum benefit from whatever activity we have chosen to do. Above all else, this must become a priority when we are involved in aerobic exercise if we are to gain maximum oxygen absorption and fat-burning potential. Simple rules include never holding the breath when working aerobically and checking that we can hold a conversation without effort or gasping for breath while we are exercising.

If we move beyond this point and find difficulty in catching our breath, we may have stopped working effectively aerobically and entered a phase of anaerobic activity, a counterproductive state for fitness because it signifies that we are not making maximum use of the oxygen that we are breathing in. Once you realise this is happening, slow down the pace until you reach the point where you can speak without strain and then maintain this level of activity for the duration of your aerobic activity.

Enhanced detoxification

Don't forget that when we breathe out we are releasing carbon dioxide from our bodies. This is a major agent of detoxification, because it expels the by-products of oxidation and energy release from the body. When we breathe out fully while exercising we are increasing the volume of oxygen we take in when we inhale, as well as utilising the amount of oxygen available to us with each inspiration. See p. 150 for general advice on breathing from the diaphragm.

Choosing the right combination of exercise

Before we can establish what sort of choice is available to us, we first need to ask ourselves some very basic questions so that we can establish our own individual fitness profile.

- First of all, we need to assess how fit we are already. There is little point in trying to train for a half marathon if we are totally unused to exercise. For basic ways of identifying your problem areas, see the all-round fitness assessment table below.
- We need to consider what form of physical activity is going to be fun for us. Without the magic ingredient of enjoyment we are going to find endless excuses for putting off exercising. Always remember that we are all individuals with our own unique temperaments and personalities. These aspects must be taken into account if exercise is going to benefit our physical, emotional and mental needs.
- The amount of time we can realistically make available is also of paramount importance. If a fitness regime is going to work, we must be sure at the outset that we can support the amount of time we propose to allocate to exercising on a long-term basis. The secret is to be modest rather than over-ambitious when we decide how much of our time can be devoted to exercise. Remember, if it's working really well, the chances are that we shall find the extra time we need. This is the best way for a more demanding schedule to develop, since steady organic growth that naturally increases in this way is more likely to continue. On the other hand, putting unrealistic demands on ourselves at the beginning is too likely to result in our giving up, however well-intentioned we may feel at the beginning.
- From the all-round fitness assessment table below identify the form of fitness activity you need the most and give it priority over other forms of exercise. In this way you can keep your fitness regime streamlined from the outset.
- Ask yourself how imaginative you were in the past, when you may have rejected the idea of exercise as not suiting your personality.

Let your imagination wander, and you might be surprised to find that you have ignored a possible activity which both suits your personality and can also boost your fitness levels.

General fitness assessment

Our first priority should be to identify any areas of our bodies that are making their presence felt. When all is working well, we should not notice how any parts of our body are functioning. Pain or discomfort are the clues our bodies will use to tell us that all is not well in a particular area. As a result, they should never be ignored.

Table 1: Fitness assessment

General problems	Fitness assessment	Suggested systems of exercise
Focus attention on your body and note any areas showing tension and stiffness. Walk about and observe how your body feels in motion: free and flexible, or tight and full of discomfort?	If a number of areas feel tight, stiff, or inflexible, it is worth concentrating on systems of movement that encourage **flexibility**.	Pilates Yoga Stretch and tone classes T'ai chi The Alexander Technique
Bend, kneel and raise yourself slowly from a sitting position. Notice whether the movements are fluid or restricted. Identify the areas that feel strained or tense. Also	Areas that feel strained and tense should benefit from a system of exercise that provides a combination of enhanced **flexibility** and **relaxation**.	Yoga Pilates T'ai chi Qi gong

General problems	Fitness assessment	Suggested systems of exercise
make a mental note of any joints that feel stiff or make cracking sounds.		The Alexander Technique
When carrying heavy bags, observe how quickly your arms feel tired. Also make a point of noticing if your legs ache after climbing an incline, or if arms continue to feel painful after carrying a heavy weight.	Problems here would suggest **lack of muscular strength** and **poor muscle tone**.	Pilates Body sculpting Aqua aerobics Yoga Weight training Swimming
When walking at a brisk pace or climbing two or three flights of stairs, observe how out of breath you become. Can you speak with ease afterwards, or are you gasping for breath? Do you feel dizzy or light-headed, or is your heartbeat excessively fast?	Any of these problems would suggest that **aerobic fitness** levels need to be improved.	Brisk walking Dancing Skipping Cycling Swimming Any sporting activity that leads to continuous, rhythmic movement which places increased demands on the heart and lungs.
Notice the area of your jaw. How tight and tense is it? When holding a pen, how tightly are you grasping it? How much tension is there in the area of the	Any tension in these areas suggests a need for activities that induce muscular, mental and emotional **relaxation**.	Autogenic training T'ai chi Qi gong Diaphragmatic breathing Yoga

General problems	Fitness assessment	Suggested systems of exercise
neck and shoulders or lower back?		The Alexander Technique. Any activity that promotes a soothing, relaxed feeling

In the following table you will find some basic suggestions about the optimum length of time you should spend at your chosen activity.

Table 2: Time spent

Nature of fitness problem	Optimum amount of time spent in fitness activity
Lack of flexibility	Aim to spend fifteen minutes at your chosen activity two or three times each week to start with. Gradually build up to thirty-five minutes of exercise which can be done four or five times a week. It helps to have at least two days a week when you don't exercise in order to let your muscles relax.
Reduced flexibility with need for relaxation	Suggested exercise activity should be done whenever you feel tense or in need of relaxation. This could involve a short ten-minute session every day, or twenty minutes of activity three times a week.
Lack of muscular strength and poor muscle tone	Aim at first for three fifteen-minute sessions of exercise a week, building up to three half-hour sessions weekly. Some of the systems mentioned, such as Yoga can be done at home once you have mastered the basic postures.

Nature of fitness problem	Optimum amount of time spent in fitness activity
Poor aerobic fitness	Beginners should build up slowly to twenty minutes of continuous activity three times a week. Don't forget that short bursts of aerobic activity can be painlessly built into your daily routine by taking the stairs instead of escalators or lifts, taking a walk at lunch-time, or walking short distances instead of using a car or taking a bus.
Lack of relaxation	See advice given for reduced flexibility with need for relaxation

Nuts and bolts advice

We now take a look at some of the most basic issues that may concern us if we are newcomers to physical fitness.

Fitness clothes

Many of us may be put off exercising by feeling that designer fitness clothes and smart gyms are not for us. Apart from anything else, we may just not be prepared for the expense that can be involved in this sort of venture. If this sounds familiar to you, think again. For most of the systems of exercise listed above and described in more detail below, we only need the minimum of exercise clothing, including the following.

- If we want to improve our aerobic performance all we really need to be concerned with is buying a good pair of walking shoes that give our feet the support they need and avoid the risk of injury. If you feel you want to invest in a pair of trainers, look for 'cross trainers' that can be used in a variety of activities. Make sure that your shoes aren't too tight for comfort or there is a strong risk that they will squeeze and distort the shape of your foot. Heel blisters can be avoided by wearing a shoe that doesn't fit too snugly or flap against the heel. Changing damp socks can also do a great deal to avoid blistering. Soles should also be flexible rather than too rigid, so that your feet can move freely and comfortably.

- A sports bra is a very worthwhile investment if you intend to run on a regular basis, especially if breasts become premenstrually enlarged and painful. Clothes should generally be loose and comfortable enough to allow for easy movement. It is generally a good idea to wear layers that can be removed or added according to whether we are getting overheated or chilled.

- When doing stretching exercises, wear clothes that feel comfortable, loose and warm. Any items of clothing that are restricting under the arms or around the neck or waist should be avoided. Loose stretch trousers, leggings or jump-suits are very suitable. If you feel that you want to invest in exercise clothes, all-in-one stretch garments are much more practical than wearing separate items such as a leotard and tights (they are also much easier and quicker to put on and take off in a hurry). Footless or stirrup garments (with a band of stretch material that fits under the foot) allow the feet to grip the floor more effectively and lessen the risk of slipping.

- The same considerations apply when we are doing relaxation techniques. It is essential to feel warm enough for the duration of our relaxation session. When we enter a state of deep relaxation our body temperature drops significantly, so we need to wear clothing that compensates for this loss of temperature. Becoming chilled when relaxing has a twofold disadvantage: we are more likely to injure or damage cold muscles (this applies in particular to activities that combine stretching and relaxation techniques) and feeling uncomfortably cold can distract us from fully relaxing. The room in which you are relaxing should also be warm enough to be comfortable, without feeling stuffy or badly-ventilated (overheated rooms can lead us to fall asleep, which is not the same as achieving a state of deep, conscious relaxation).

Class-based exercise versus exercising at home

When we set out to master a new form of exercise, it is worth making the effort to attend a class. The reason for this is simple and the key to success: it is crucially important to learn the basics of an exercise system under the tuition and guidance of a trained teacher with the necessary experience to protect you against doing anything likely to result in injury. A responsible teacher is able to tailor a class to the abilities of its participants and, ideally, ask any new members if they are suffering from any medical problems that might have a bearing on what they should attempt. For this reason, it is always a good idea to have a private word with your teacher before a class begins if you suffer from joint problems, back pain, high or low blood pressure, or asthma.

Once you have become familiar with an exercise system (such as Yoga, T'ai chi, or a stretch class) through attending a class for a while, whether or not you continue going to class or work at home is really up to your individual temperament. Some people severely miss the motivation of attending a regular class, and find it almost impossible to keep up the same commitment at home alone. Others also miss the conviviality and social interaction of mixing with others in a class, especially if they work from home and tend to feel socially quite isolated.

Other forms of exercise also demand the use of specialised equipment to which we cannot have access at home; these include weight training which uses static machines rather than hand-held weights, Pilates studio equipment (although this form of exercise can also be taught without these machines) and access to a swimming pool.

Arguments in favour of working at home include the flexibility and freedom of being able to choose for ourselves when we exercise; the overall reduction of time spent in preparation and after exercise (this can be especially relevant to those for whom time is at a premium), and the basic psychological reality that some people don't work well in a group activity and feel much more at ease exercising at home at their own pace.

Maintaining an exercise regime at home has also been given a boost by the advent of the exercise video. Although they do have their limitations and drawbacks, exercise videos have become the bridge between the formality and structure of attending a class and the lack of clarity and confusion that can often arise from using an exercise textbook or audio cassette tape at home.

On the other hand, it is also important to point out that not all exercise videos are desirable; some have been criticised for including exercises that are unsafe, or not giving enough advice to those who should avoid certain postures. This is yet another reason for making sure that you attend a class initially. By doing so, you can develop a basic knowledge and familiarity with the exercise system involved, which will probably enable you to gain more from using a video at home. One of the advantages of using an exercise video on a regular basis is that it can overcome the problem of lack of motivation when exercising at home, because the video should take you through a structured routine which enables you just to follow along rather than have to think out your own exercise routine every time.

Warming up and cooling down

If we want to gain maximum benefit from exercising, we need to understand why it is absolutely essential to warm up before and cool down after exercise. Limbering up considerably reduces the risk of injury; too many sports injuries are caused by using muscles that are either too cold or not sufficiently relaxed. This is particularly true of stretching activities intended to be steadily built up in intensity and repetition, because it enables the muscles to take the stretch more easily and cumulatively as we gain in flexibility.

Warming up is also an excellent way of preparing the mind for activity as we gently ease ourselves into exercise, otherwise it can feel quite an abrupt shock to the system. On the other hand, this needn't be taken to extremes. For instance, if we are about to take a brisk walk there obviously is no need for any special preparation: we just need to put our shoes on and go!

Cooling down is even more important, especially after aerobic activity that has worked the heart and lungs. No aerobic activity should ever be stopped abruptly; the pace should be slowly and steadily reduced to give us a chance to regulate our breathing rate and patterns as we slow down. In this way, our lungs and hearts are less likely to be required to make a rapid and demanding adjustment. Just like a warm up, a cool down session gives us an opportunity to mark the conclusion to our exercise activity and become mentally prepared for whatever task we are about to do next. This is particularly true after we have engaged in deep relaxation; ideally we should resume activity gently and slowly rather than rushing things. This is important because otherwise we are likely to lose the benefits gained from the deep relaxation.

Exercise and weight loss

If we are concerned about weight loss, it helps to understand at the outset that the rate at which we gain or lose weight is fundamentally determined by our metabolic rate. The latter establishes the rate at which we burn up the food we take in. In other words, if this rate is sluggish or slow (even if the food we eat is low in calorific value), any food that isn't used for heat and energy production will be stored and laid down as deposits of fat.

On the other hand, when we have a high metabolic rate, we could take in an identical amount of food but find that our body burns up the calorific intake much more efficiently. As a result, there will be little food left for laying down fatty deposits and weight levels will remain more stable or on the lower side.

Because of the importance of our metabolic rates, contemporary advice on weight loss increasingly emphasises the central importance of the role played by an efficient and well-balanced metabolism, rather than emphasising calorie-controlled diets alone. Strictly controlling calorific intake is now seen as a far from efficient long-term strategy for effective weight loss because, although calorie-controlled diets can at first enable us to lose weight, most of us will discover that we rapidly hit a plateau where our weight remains infuriatingly and stubbornly the same, even though we still carefully restrict our food intake.

The good news, however, is that we can do a great deal to kick-start and speed up our metabolic rate by exercising on a regular basis. By doing this, we can speed up weight loss and improve our body shape, provided we make sure that we combine a regular exercise regime with an eating plan that is low in refined sugar and fat, but high in complex carbohydrates and whole foods. In order for this effect to be maintained, it is essential that we engage regularly in the exercise we choose. It is less beneficial to set aside an hour every fortnight than enjoy a minimum of twenty or thirty minutes of exercise three times a week.

Once physical fitness becomes a regular feature of daily life it has the added bonus of modifying the ratio of muscle to fat in our bodies in favour of muscle. This is why, although many of us may look more slender and lean when we keep up a regular exercise regime, our weight remains much the same, or in some cases may even increase by one or two pounds. This occurs because muscle is heavier than fat, with the result that as muscles are toned and conditioned they actually begin to weigh more than flabby and out of condition muscles. At the same time, as our muscles become better defined, we should find that inches begin to disappear from our waist, hips and thighs.

Too much of a good thing: exercise addiction

In just the same way that eating disorders became a focus of attention in the 1980s, the issue of exercise addiction is gaining more attention in the late 1990s.

We can be helped to gain an insight into the latter by identifying the links between exercise addiction and eating disorders. Both problems tend to affect the lives of those who have a lingering dissatisfaction with their body image, but the following features also tend to be shared by sufferers from both exercise addiction and eating disorders:

- Low self-esteem and poor self-confidence
- Fear of failure
- Perfectionist and highly competitive tendencies
- An overwhelming need to be in control
- Problems in establishing and maintaining close relationships

Exercise addiction could be regarded as a phenomenon that flourished in the tough and harsh competitive atmosphere that pervaded the popular model of exercise in the 1980s. This uncompromising and punishing approach to fitness encouraged the degree of disruption and isolation involved in exercise addiction. In the same way that a bulimic or anorexic person goes to frightening lengths in order to maintain their addiction, an obsessive weight trainer or runner puts keeping up an exercise regime before any other priority. In this situation, not even an injury would stand in the way of a true addict: you may have heard examples of serious runners who felt compelled to run even when they were in extreme pain from an actual or threatened injury.

Exercise addiction is an excellent example of how something that in itself is health-promoting can become the absolute opposite when perception of it gets out of balance. Sadly, once it has reached the stage of obsession, addiction to exercise becomes destructive in nature rather than life affirming.

As a gentler and more rounded approach to exercise has developed through the 1990s, it is to be hoped that exercise addiction will come to be seen as totally at odds with the basic philosophy of holism, with its emphasis on working with the body, rather than subduing it. Unfortunately, addiction to exercise is the very opposite of a balanced and integrated approach to fitness, because it is stress-creating rather than stress-diminishing. This is especially true if exercise is denied for any significant length of time.

It is important to appreciate that exercise in itself is not the problem; it is the attitude brought to it that determines whether things are in balance or not. The following can be taken as basic indications that an over-commitment to exercise is building up difficulties and a phase of imbalance is beginning:

- Total priority is given to exercise at the expense of other commitments, including family or social life.
- Profound or overwhelming guilt, anger, or extreme restlessness is experienced if exercise is prevented.
- Increasing dissatisfaction with body image or fitness levels leads to pushing boundaries and goalposts further and further, especially if this is linked to restricting food intake.
- There is noticeable self-preoccupation and isolation.

We need to approach exercise as a tool which, like sound nutrition or relaxation, can be used as a way of enhancing our lives and making them more rounded. However, an obsessive approach to anything prevents us from experiencing the full range of emotional and physical health. The answer lies not in avoiding or being wary of exercise, but in establishing a new perspective and model for exercising that celebrates its positive and life-enhancing qualities.

A quick tour of some exercise systems

This section includes some very well-known forms of exercise, as well as some that may be less familiar. This is not intended to be an exhaustive or comprehensive explanation of each method, but more of a thumbnail sketch that gives a basic introduction to each system.

Pilates (pronounced Pill-ah-tays)

The Pilates method was devised in the 1920s but it has experienced a fresh lease of life over the past decade. Originally developed as a physiotherapeutic method, Pilates emphasises the development of a keen sense of body awareness while exercising. In recent years it has become established as a form of exercise with the potential for an increasingly broad application and popularity.

Attention began to be focused on this system of physical fitness when it was revealed that it had been used by the French actor

Christopher Lambert when he needed to develop an impressive physique for his role in the film *Greystoke*. When other high-profile celebrities such as Marie Helvin were mentioned in connection with the Pilates technique, the inevitable magazine features appeared as well as books aimed at a new audience.

Because the basic exercise techniques involved are tailored to suit the needs of the individual, Pilates does not force anyone to pursue a posture with which they feel ill at ease or uncomfortable. As a result, this is an exercise technique which promotes muscle strength, reduces stress, increases flexibility and draws attention to poor postural habits that may unknowingly have been adopted over the years in response to stress.

In many ways, Pilates classes provide a perfect example of the opposite approach to the high impact, punishing, competitive, furiously-paced communal classes mentioned previously. This is because the successful use of the Pilates technique involves precise, conscious working of isolated muscles for a limited number of repetitions. In order to achieve maximum accuracy in learning the exercises, tuition tends to be given on an individual basis within the context of a class of strictly limited numbers.

Those of us who are concerned about looking 'muscle bound' need not worry when it comes to the Pilates technique. Although the exercises will strengthen weak muscles and stretch tight ones, they will not lead to our developing bulky, over-developed muscles. On the contrary, overall muscle tone should be improved as the body appears taller and more slender as a direct result of improved alignment and posture.

Pilates exercises can also help us to escape the common trap of high repetition of exercises in the hope that they are doing some good. This is because the Pilates technique demands a high level of concentration if the exercises are to be done correctly and the greatest benefits obtained. The degree of attention that is brought to the exercises encourages us to focus on how our bodies are reacting, which gives us a keener sense of the benefits we are reaping from exercising.

Because of the need for accuracy in doing Pilates exercises in order to obtain maximum benefit, there is no substitute for initially attending a class with a trained teacher. Once they are well mastered, these exercises can then be done at home with the help of one of the self-help video tapes available on the market.

Yoga

When we speak about Yoga in the West, we are normally referring to Hatha Yoga. This is a centuries-old system of exercise that emphasises the need for each posture (*asana*) to be done in harmony with breath control (*pranayama*). The word Yoga can be loosely translated from Sanskrit to mean 'the union of body and mind'. The regular practice of Yoga is believed to balance energies in the body so that physical, emotional and mental resilience is increased.

One of the main principles of Yoga suggests that working on the body comes before working on the mind. Hatha Yoga is regarded as enabling us to develop a finer sense of consciousness through initially developing the body, with the result that it concentrates very much on physical development of strength and suppleness. This form of exercise includes fluid movements and demanding stretches that have the positive result of stimulating energy levels, promoting stamina and encouraging better muscle tone.

In addition, those who practise Yoga are taught how to breathe correctly in order to relax or stimulate energy levels and improve the depth of stretching. As a result, Yoga is very challenging to master but can yield startling results in terms of increased vitality and a vastly improved sense of well-being.

Yoga is an especially appropriate and liberating option for those who may have been alienated from exercise in their youth or early teens by a spartan, or overly-competitive atmosphere or conditions. For those of us who feel this way, it is a refreshing revelation to discover that when we practise Yoga we are in competition with absolutely no-one but ourselves. As a result, we should never be required to force our bodies beyond any point with which we do not feel comfortable.

This is especially relevant to those with limitations on their fitness level or flexibility, since many Yoga postures can be modified to meet individual limitations.

In addition, because this system of exercise has at its core the philosophy that we are striving for maximum harmony between body and mind, a developing sense of body awareness can guard against our injuring ourselves by pushing our bodies beyond a pain barrier. The postures are done consciously, carefully and slowly in order to minimise the risk of damaging any part of our bodies as a result of jerking or pulling muscles in an abrupt or violent way.

Learning how to breathe well also helps us unwind and let go when we are feeling under stress. Using relaxing breathing techniques is not restricted to a Yoga class; once we have mastered how to breathe for relaxation, we can use it any time we feel anxious or stressed.

When setting out to learn Yoga, it is essential to attend a class in order to learn how to accomplish some basic postures and master diaphragmatic breathing techniques for relaxation. This is very important, because there is little point in trying to practise at home if we are not executing the postures properly. Always remember that maximum benefit can only be derived from doing the postures as carefully and accurately as possible (this is also less likely to result in injury).

However, once we are familiar and confident with what we are doing, there is no reason not to continue practising at home. Using a Yoga home video recommended by a teacher can provide excellent help by giving us a structure and boundaries within which we can work comfortably. This can be quite refreshing, because it takes the pressure off our having to determine our own routine for practice. A Yoga teacher should also recommend home practice and produce a worksheet to follow.

T'ai chi ch'uan (pronounced Tie chee chwan)

In T'ai chi slow, graceful movements and breathing techniques are used to stimulate the flow of energy (*chi*) through the body. The overall effect of these movements is to promote a general sense of calm and stimulate physical resilience.

T'ai chi can be used as a non-combative martial art for self-defence, in addition to its potential as a healing system for promoting a sense of mental and emotional clarity. It is thought to encourage the healthy flow of chi through the meridians (channels of energy that acupuncturists believe traverse the body). Research has revealed that T'ai chi exercises relax the muscles and nervous system, as well as improving all-round flexibility, posture and balance. In addition, as a system of movement it appears to have the benefit of maximising breathing efficiency without putting undue strain on the heart.

As with Yoga, it is best to attend classes with a teacher in order to master the basic postures thoroughly and at the optimum pace. The size of a class can vary from one-to-one tuition to groups of fifteen or twenty. As with a Yoga class, it is best to inform your teacher at the beginning of any medical conditions which are currently a problem. Clothes should be comfortable and loose, and shoes should be comfortable and flat-soled, to allow your feet to keep contact with the surface of the floor. Trainers are unfortunately not suitable, partly because of the thickness of the soles.

Classes should feel relaxed and unhurried, putting a strong emphasis on breathing that encourages a relaxed, almost meditative state. Ideally, aim to practise each day; weekly sessions should be regarded as the absolute minimum to aim for in order to gain maximum benefit. Once mastered, video tapes are available that can take us through a guided class, but these should not be relied on as a method by which to learn the technique of Ta'i chi.

Qi gong (pronounced Chee gong)

Qi gong has been described as a form of meditation in movement. Like T'ai chi, the postures used in Qi gong are believed to have the beneficial effect of stimulating the balanced flow of chi energy throughout the body. It is thought that observing the instinctive and fluid movements of wild animals helped to provide the inspiration for the movements in Qi gong.

Loosely translated, the words Qi gong describe the cultivation and conservation of *qi* (vital energy). It can be regarded as a system of bodily movement intimately linked to the general approach of traditional Chinese medicine, because of its emphasis on the importance of promoting the healthy and balanced flow of life energy.

One of the core aspects of Qi gong embraces the overriding need for balance and harmony in the body as a whole, as well as a developed sense of awareness of the centre of the body. Once these dual abilities are within our grasp, we have the optimum chance of harmonising the flow of qi within our bodies. When we have reached this state, our energy levels should be at their most balanced, while emotional and mental well-being should also reflect this basic state of harmony.

From the perspective of traditional Chinese medicine, taking personal responsibility for the prevention of illness through the promotion of mental, emotional, and physical well-being is of paramount importance if we are to live in harmony with the way of Nature (often referred to as the Tao). From this fundamentally holistic perspective, if we are to live life to the full we must avoid overwork, becoming unduly stressed, having an unbalanced diet, and following a lifestyle that is primarily sedentary and lacking in regular exercise.

On the other hand, if we rectify these imbalances by improving our diet, reducing stress, pacing ourselves and using acupuncture (or other forms of alternative medicine that are believed to work by stimulating the body's capacity for self-healing) and the practice of Qi gong to regulate our energy levels, we have a fighting chance of enjoying an optimum sense of well-being and vitality.

In Qi gong, certain parts of the body are endowed with a special significance and importance. These areas include the crown of the head, the brow, the tongue, heart, navel, palms of the hands, soles of the feet and the perineum. By becoming conscious of these areas and controlling the intake and release of the breath, it is thought that we can enhance our mental, emotional and physical strength, vitality, and resilience.

As with Yoga and T'ai chi, it is important to obtain initial tuition in Qi gong from a trained practitioner who can teach us how to perform the postures correctly with regard to pace and positioning of the body. Once learned accurately, there is no reason why this technique cannot be used at home. Further information may be obtained from some of the self-help books on this subject which are now on the market.

The Alexander Technique

Although it is not an exercise system, the Alexander Technique should be included in any discussion of the issue of building body awareness through movement. The Alexander Technique can benefit anyone who feels ill at ease with their body, or who may have become aware of specific postural problems that may have developed over the years. These can often become apparent due to unwelcome and persistent pain in the neck, back, or shoulders.

The Alexander Technique teaches us that the way we hold our bodies unconsciously reflects how we feel emotionally, especially if we are under severe or constant emotional stress. By identifying these habits and opening up the possibility of change, the Alexander Technique can free us from instinctive, ingrained patterns of emotional behaviour. This is done by developing an awareness of our physical reactions when we are faced with people or situations that we perceive to be stressful or threatening. Once we have an insight into the instinctive physical reactions we employ in difficult surroundings, we can learn a great deal about what we sacrifice in order to cope with these situations, and decide for ourselves if another way might not be easier and better for us.

Once we have gained these insights into our postural habits they can be of immense value in making us more aware of how our bodies respond to movement. This can have the knock-on effect of enriching our experience while we exercise, making it less likely that we will injure ourselves as a result of forcing our bodies into inappropriate or uncomfortable postures.

Emotional experience and posture

It is fascinating to watch what happens to our bodies each time we feel depressed, anxious, or stressed. When we feel down, this is often literally reflected in the way we hold ourselves: our shoulders often droop, and our bodies look and feel as if everything is dragging and sagging downwards. On the other hand, when we are tense and anxious we are likely to notice that our jaws are clenched tight, the muscles in our neck, shoulders and upper back are tense and rigid and we may feel aches and pains in any of these areas. Since maintaining these postural distortions uses up a great deal of energy, there is a good chance that we also feel weary, lethargic and lacking in sparkle as a direct result of the posture we adopt under emotional pressure.

However, this is just the negative side of the picture. Once it is reversed we can begin the exciting journey of discovery in which we learn how awareness of our postural reactions can help us when we find ourselves in situations which feel anxiety-making or depressing. By becoming more in tune with our bodies and learning how to loosen up physically and relax, we shall often find that we can combat feelings of anxiety or depression. Put slightly differently, if we can influence our posture by how we feel, we can equally affect how we feel by altering our posture.

Be aware that long-established, ingrained postural habits can take a long time to break; initially, better postural alignment can feel uncomfortable and strange. As a result, we may spend a lot of our time instinctively longing to return to what feels familiar and superficially more comfortable to us, regardless of the damage it may be doing. The important thing to remember is that we can use our awareness of our body to help us in situations of emotional crisis by developing a keen awareness of the signals it is sending us, rather than constantly bracing and arming ourselves against tension, only to wonder later why we feel so tense and exhausted.

The Alexander Technique must be learnt from a trained teacher rather than attempting to learn the technique by ourselves from a book. Classes are usually given on a one-to-one basis, with a large part of the time being spent observing the way we use our bodies when we do simple movements such as sitting or raising ourselves out of a chair. Once tuition is well under way, an Alexander teacher may well suggest exercises to develop our experience of the technique at home.

5

Mental and Emotional Boosters

How often can we say that we feel truly alive, the world around us looks vibrant, our energy levels soar and we feel that we want to sing from sheer happiness? If we are exceptionally lucky, we may know this experience very well, but for many of us it is too fleeting a sensation. We may have had a taste of this magical state of mind when something wonderful happens, like falling in love, achieving something special, or escaping from day-to-day pressures on a spellbinding holiday. Unfortunately, most of these experiences are short-lived, leaving us with the problem of adjusting to 'normal' everyday life once they are over. For many of us the possible options include trying to duplicate the missing emotional high by seeking to repeat the experience, or having to be content with just getting by most of the time.

There is, however, an alternative option that we shall be exploring in this section of the six-point plan. This is the possibility of finding ways of boosting our mental and emotional capacity for balance and harmony, so that we are freed from the constraints of being dependent upon external triggers for excitement, contentment, or happiness. Once we have developed this potential within ourselves, it can have an extraordinarily positive effect on our overall level of health.

A holistic approach to health

For many of us, thinking about achieving optimum health is limited to aiming for maximum energy levels and absence of physical symptoms of illness. However, high-quality health is much, much more, since mental and emotional balance and harmony lie at the root of a truly vibrant sense of well-being. In others words, when we experience our optimum potential for vitality, our levels of confidence, concentration, zest for life, and ability to relax and unwind should all be increased to their maximum.

Perhaps this sounds a little too much like a state of Nirvana which it would be very nice to achieve, but is surely a bit too unrealistic when we live and work in the real world with all its attendant stresses, strains and heartaches? If this downbeat approach sounds familiar to you, think again. Once we pay attention to our mental and emotional health and take the necessary steps to nurture and protect them, we are likely to be amazed at the results that follow.

In this section we shall be exploring the steps we can all take in order to give ourselves the best possible chance of experiencing freedom from negative stress, anxiety and mental and emotional sluggishness or fatigue. We shall explore the tools we need to have at our disposal for avoiding mental and emotional burn out and coming to terms with the negative or fearful thought patterns that may be preventing us from moving on with our lives. Perhaps most important of all, these tools will help us to feel that we are 'in the driving seat' once again (or perhaps for the first time). In other words, we shall begin to experience the exhilarating sensation that we are making our own choices about how we live our lives, rather than feeling that life is something that just happens to us as passive observers.

The alternative medical perspective

Ask any experienced alternative therapist about the importance of the role played by our mental and emotional balance in establishing and maintaining optimum health, and they should reply that it is absolutely crucial. In other words, it is very rare for an alternative practitioner to meet a patient who is seeking treatment for a host of well-established physical symptoms, who feels that they have masses of emotional and mental energy. Most patients, when asked how well they feel generally since developing their illness, usually complain of feeling stressed, wrung out, lacking in confidence, anxious, depressed, or lacking in clarity or focus. Often, it is a question of experiencing a combination of many of these before the symptoms of physical illness make themselves apparent.

This link between our mental and emotional and physical health is partly acknowledged by conventional doctors, who recognise that a range of stress-related illnesses exist that appear to be positively, or adversely, affected by emotional health or general state of mind. Irritable bowel syndrome, asthma, eczema, migraines and stomach ulcers are just some of the medical conditions that appear to be brought on, or aggravated by, an excess of mental and emotional stress.

Many alternative practitioners, however, go a step further, and see links between a wider range of conditions and compromised experience of mental and emotional well-being. In my own experience as a homoeopath, I have seen patients who have presented with symptoms of rheumatoid arthritis after unexpressed grief, or recurrent infections such as cystitis following a severe emotional shock or trauma. In cases such as these it is as if the mind registers and suffers trauma first, with physical symptoms emerging at a later date, rather like ripples which radiate very slowly outwards as a delayed reaction after the original contact.

Thus, when improvement takes place as a result of successful treatment, it is not uncommon for patients to claim that they feel much more positive and energised in themselves before their physical symptoms have improved. In other words, they may still have their physical problems, but they feel less distressed by them. When this reaction occurs as a result of homoeopathic treatment, the physical symptoms will also clear up in reverse order of their appearance. From a holistic perspective, cure is not merely assessed by the absence of physical symptoms, but can only be regarded as happening when mind, emotions and body are restored to their optimum balance for each individual.

However, rather than letting problems build to a point where symptoms of illness set in and professional help is needed, the following section will guide us through some practical steps we can take in order to protect our mental and emotional well-being when life seems too tough.

Stress: mental and emotional enemy number one

Stress seems to be the buzz word on everybody's lips these days. How do we identify it, what do we do with it, and how can we escape it? Some people argue that we should do all in our power to eliminate this disease-inducing element from our lives, while others are adamant that stress gives us the edge we need to keep sharp and energised.

In reality it helps enormously if we regard stress as neutral in itself; it is often the way we react to it that determines its effect on us. It is also rather misleading and unproductive to talk about stress as a blanket term, because we shall probably get much further if we try to differentiate between positive and negative stress. Positive stress is often short-term, triggered by something that challenges us or puts us on the spot such as sitting an examination or meeting a pressing deadline. If we are well prepared to meet these challenges, this is the sort of stress that brings out the best in us by getting us motivated and thinking sharply. The favourable result should be that we perform well for the task in hand and can unwind and relax once the challenge has been met and the pressure is off. When we respond to these circumstances, our minds and responses become rapid and sharp and we may feel the exhilaration of working at a level of clarity that we cannot achieve on a day-to-day basis.

Negative stress, however, is the flip side or mirror image of this positive picture. It tends to involve long-term situations and often results in the building of a slow sensation of mental, emotional and physical tension that can erupt at intervals into feelings of absolute blind panic or extreme anger and irritability. This form of stress is the absolute opposite of the positive variety, because it is essentially counterproductive in the way that it muddles and confuses mental clarity. As a result, when we experience negative stress we become the opposite of mentally sharper, often finding decisions much harder to make. In essence, situations involving negative stress tend to make us feel powerless and the opposite of being in control, with the result that our sense of self-esteem and levels of self-confidence become adversely affected. Good examples of situations involving negative stress would include sitting an examination or giving a presentation for which we are badly prepared, or facing financial problems that do not seem to have a feasible solution.

Some common symptoms of negative stress

- Mental and physical sensations of tension, restlessness and general uneasiness
- Light or easily disturbed sleep
- Severe mood swings, including swift onset of anxiety and irritability
- Feeling unable to cope and overwhelmed by even the smallest or simplest of tasks

- Panic attacks
- Palpitations
- Digestive disturbances including nausea, lack of appetite, indigestion, heartburn, diarrhoea, or constipation
- Comfort eating, or revulsion at the thought, sight, or smell of food
- Recurrent headaches and/or migraines
- Lack of energy
- Poor skin tone and skin quality
- Relying on stimulants such as coffee in order to keep going, and alcohol in order to wind down and relax.

Energy-draining aspects of negative stress

In many ways, a long period of negative stress is one of the greatest threats to feelings of vitality, because counterproductive stress depletes our energy levels without our being consciously aware of this happening. In the same way that long-drawn-out pain or anxiety leaves us feeling physically shattered, having to cope with negative stress produces a very similar scenario. In addition, the situation is often made much worse because it is very difficult to make eating well a priority when under strain, although it is exactly at times of severe stress that we need a plentiful supply of essential nutrients such as the B vitamins and the mineral magnesium, to support our nervous systems.

Extra problems that may also compromise our levels of energy and vitality include the link between stress levels and the likelihood of constipation, and recurrent digestive problems such as indigestion and acidity: these can be made worse by the tendency when stressed to over-rely on 'quick-fix' junk foods. Smoking also depletes the body of essential nutrients and at the same time exposes the body to free radicals, while over-consumption of alcohol when stressed has an adverse effect on our digestive systems, sleep pattern, emotions (it is a depressant) and skin quality. If we add into the equation additional possible problems such as stiffness and aches and pains in muscles and joints through constant muscular tension, clearly stress of this kind can be a major obstacle when we want to feel energised and on top form.

Simple tricks for diffusing stress

The following suggestions are just some of the positive steps that we can take to manage stress levels in our lives. As a result of taking control and adopting some of these suggestions, we can begin to manage the stress in our lives effectively, rather than feeling that stress is managing us.

Identifying priorities

When feeling overwhelmed by the amount of work to be done, making a list of what has to be done in order of priority can instantly diminish the scale of the problem and make it more manageable. Although it sounds obvious, organising our thoughts in this way can stop us feeling as though we can't see the wood for the trees. It is essential to avoid this, because feeling bogged-down can leave us confused, indecisive and more stressed than ever, so that nothing much gets done and we may be left feeling generally tense and guilty. However, when we put the activities we need to tackle down on paper, this immediately makes them less threatening and tasks that require obvious priority tend to stand out. Listing things on paper also has the important effect of focusing the mind, helping us to think more clearly about what we should do. The tasks that require immediate attention should occupy the top position on the list, while less pressing jobs should appear further down. It also helps to note whether a job needs to be done immediately, or can be delayed for a short or longer time. There may be some tasks that don't need to be tackled at all, or can be handled effectively by others. Once a job has been dealt with, make sure it is crossed off the list: it's amazing how therapeutic it can be to see a list like this getting shorter.

Paying attention to organising our surroundings

When we are feeling that it's really just too difficult to cope, it can be surprisingly revealing and illuminating to stop for a moment and look around at the immediate surroundings in which we work. For many of us, our external environment reflects our state of mind: in other words, when we are feeling mentally disorganised and over-whelmed by the scale of what we have to do, this sensation can often be reinforced by physically being surrounded by clutter and disorganised heaps of books and paper. Conversely, once we get to grips with organising our professional and/or home surroundings, it becomes much easier to work efficiently and with enthusiasm. Apart from anything else, it's so much easier to get down to creatively-flowing work when we can find the material we need quickly and easily, rather than wasting time and energy on searching through endless disorganised heaps of paper. Just to give a simple example: it's far easier to find a document that has been put in an appropriate file than one that is buried under a mountain of junk. Finding something that is needed quickly without effort also bypasses the frustration and irritation that inevitably arises if we lose an important reference when we are under pressure.

However, as always, we need to strike a healthy balance, since a preoccupation with neatness and organisation can become unhealthy if it reaches a point of obsession. When this happens, the desire to maintain order and control can take over from the importance of the work itself. This, unfortunately, has the negative effect of putting more emphasis and energy into the preparation for work than into the work itself.

Once we are able to bring a balanced approach to keeping order, it becomes a helpful and flexible tool that can assist us in getting on with life and creative work more easily and rewardingly. As a result, it can be a tool of immense value in diffusing stress levels and preventing us from putting things off indefinitely.

Delegating

This gets much easier once we have organised our commitments on paper, since the very action of prioritising a list of tasks draws our attention to the jobs that can be done perfectly well by someone else. Once we see this and ask for help, we can feel immensely liberated. It is also a pleasure and relief to discover that we are not as indispensable as we may have thought. Although it can be difficult initially to let go of certain tasks, once the skills of effective delegating are learnt they can reduce our stress levels virtually overnight.

Making time for ourselves

However indulgent it may sound, we should make a point of setting aside some time for ourselves every day away from the demands of others. This is perhaps the most important way we have of reducing stress levels, especially if we care for young children and close elderly relatives in addition to having a demanding job. We shouldn't make the common mistake of being too ambitious and thinking that, because we don't have hours to spare, there's no point in trying. All we actually need is five or ten minutes to ourselves when we are very busy, or as long as half an hour when we have more time to spare. Whatever resources are available, we should make this our time when we can do whatever helps us feel relaxed and refreshed. We should choose anything that suits us as individuals: soaking in an aromatic bath, walking in the fresh air, listening to favourite pieces of music, or even sitting for a while and doing absolutely nothing. Never underestimate the stress-relieving potential of spending time with a pet, either, because a relationship of this kind can have a hugely beneficial effect on anyone who feels isolated, tense or unhappy. Many of my own patients have revealed that they are able to confide in their pet cats or dogs in a frank way that they might not adopt with a human. Of course, they don't expect a verbal answer, but they find that very often verbalising a thought has its own positive value that doesn't require a reply. There is also the sheer sensual and comforting pleasure of having physical contact with a warm, furry, soft, affectionate creature. In itself, this can work wonders when we are feeling lonely or miserable.

Eating habits and stress

The digestive problems associated with a stressed lifestyle can be kept to a minimum if we make a few simple adjustments to the way we eat. Foods that commonly contribute to digestive disturbances such as indigestion should be kept to a minimum; these include any of the following:

- Raw onions
- Raw or hot chilli peppers
- Strong tea or coffee
- Spicy dishes such as hot curries
- Spirits
- Fatty foods, including full-fat cheeses, red meat and creamy sauces.

It is also helpful to avoid eating 'on the run', or when we feel tense, angry, or upset – whether we are stressed or not, digestion is always likely to happen more smoothly and easily if we take our time to relax and enjoy what we are eating.

Constipation can be one of the major problems associated with a stressful lifestyle and it can result in any of us looking and feeling wretched. Simple ways of avoiding this problem include making sure that we eat enough high-fibre foods every day, drinking a minimum of four or five large glasses of filtered tap water or still mineral water a day, and avoiding too many processed and refined foods.

Exercise and stress

Exercise can be an invaluable tool in helping to diffuse negative stress and tension. On the other hand, always remember that it's very important to avoid falling into the trap of becoming too involved in a form of exercise that is excessively competitive or addictive. Sadly, the latter can result in making us feel even more tense in the long term.

Whatever type of exercise we choose, it should, above all, be enjoyable and conducive to helping us relax and unwind afterwards. If, on the other hand, we feel more uptight after exercising than we did when we began, the chances are that we need to look elsewhere for positive results. A strong indicator that we have found the best form of activity for ourselves is that we find our minds switching off easily before sleep, and our bodies feeling at ease and relaxed. Specific exercise systems that claim to help us achieve a state of relaxation include Yoga, Pilates, and T'ai chi.

Relaxation and meditation techniques

As the pace of our lives speeds up and becomes more demanding, it is essential that we make space within which our minds and bodies can unwind. If we make the effort to do this, the benefits are enormous: we are likely to find that we can think more clearly, our energy levels are higher and we will generally experience an increased sense of well-being and vitality.

In the same way that our bodies must have regular periods of rest in order to recharge themselves to meet the daily demands and challenges, our minds must also be given space to off-load the stresses, strains and pressures that are so often involved in an average hectic day.

How to set about it

- Always make sure that regularly achieving a good quality night's sleep is the norm. The optimum amount of sleep needed will vary for each of us, but most of us will instinctively know the average amount of hours of rest we need in order to function at our very best. If sleep pattern or sleep quality has become a problem, see the 'Insomnia' section on p. 160.
- Correct breathing is an essential aid to relaxation: learning to breathe from the diaphragm helps considerably when we are feeling anxious or stressed. For basic advice on how to achieve double-quick relaxation from simple breathing techniques see the 'Anxiety' section on p. 149.

- Taking regular exercise that involves spending time in the fresh air (brisk walking or cycling) can do a great deal to help us relax when we are feeling tense. Aerobic exercise of this kind helps burn off the excess adrenalin that can build up if we have a stressful sedentary job that does not allow us to blow off steam physically when we need to.
- Make a point of combining pleasures that contribute to feelings of relaxation so that you can have double the benefit: for example, why not indulge in relaxing breathing techniques while wallowing in a soothing bath, with relaxing music playing in the background?
- Don't be afraid to use aromatherapy oils creatively; their use can include home-made massage oils, scented baths (always remember to add them very sparingly, using a maximum of five to six drops of oil), or burning in special vaporisers which release a steady scent of essential oil. Some appropriate oils to choose from include lavender, geranium and bergamot.

Relaxation techniques

Some of us may be very good at instinctively switching off whenever we need to relax . However, those of us who find relaxing an uphill struggle may benefit greatly from following a specific method of relaxation such as the simple exercise given below.

Autogenic training

This is a simple method of relaxation that teaches us how to exercise control over feelings of panic or anxiety and encourages us to reach a state of deep relaxation. Once this technique is mastered, even functions of the body that are not considered to be under our conscious control can also benefit from a relaxed state. Good examples of these involuntary functions include increased control over pulse or heart rate.

When setting out to learn this technique, it is best to be trained by a skilled practitioner in autogenic training rather than trying to teach yourself. The reason for this is very straightforward: learning the method involves mastering six simple mental exercises, which suggest that certain specific sensations are being experienced by the body, such as a feeling of warmth, heaviness, or calmness. Since some psychological reactions may occur in response to autogenic training, it is best if the support and training of a skilled and experienced practitioner is on hand to evaluate such a reaction at whatever stage it occurs.

Once learnt, autogenic training can be used to trigger a deeply relaxed state within a comparatively short space of time. Perhaps most important of all, the technique is very practical and simple and can be practised without any paraphernalia or fuss. As a result, it can be used anywhere and at any time we feel comfortable and relaxed. However, it does need to be practised regularly, so that we can develop the keen sense of physical observation that comes as we experience different sensations in a state of deep relaxation.

Meditation

Learning how to meditate can help us switch off mentally and emotionally when we feel everything is just getting too much for us to cope with. Practised daily, meditation appears to make us calmer on a emotional, mental and physical level, and it can also improve our concentration for mental tasks.

In order to achieve a meditative state, sit in a comfortable chair in a peaceful room, making sure as you sit that your spine is as straight as possible. Try to empty your mind of distracting or disturbing thoughts by focusing on an image: either something that is sitting in front of you (this could be a flower or a candle), or simply a mental image that you have chosen. Alternatively, try closing your eyes and repeat a sound to yourself over and over again. This could be as simple as repeating the word 'one' or any other sound that appeals to you as you take time to observe and regulate your breathing pattern. If distracting thoughts enter your mind (and this will happen a lot at first), don't panic, just mentally push them gently to one side and refocus your attention on your chosen image or sound.

A simple relaxation technique

In order to enjoy the maximum benefit from the following relaxation exercise, set aside half an hour each day when you know you will be able to do this free from interruption.

- Dress in loose, comfortable clothes that make you feel free and unrestricted.
- Your surroundings need to be comfortably warm but not too stuffy. Always bear in mind that your body temperature will drop when relaxing, and you need to avoid feeling chilled because this has the unwanted effect of making us anything but relaxed.
- Lie on your back on the floor (carpet is fine, or you can choose to lie on an exercise mat or towel for comfort). Bend your knees with your feet resting on the floor about a foot apart from each other. Placing one hand on your belly, feel the breath pushing your abdomen up and outwards as you breathe in, and resting back to its original position as you breathe out.
- Your breathing pattern shouldn't feel forced: just let it take its own rhythm and establish its own pattern and regularity. All you need to do is observe what is happening. (For additional advice on breathing correctly from the diaphragm, see p. 150.)
- Once you are breathing from the area around your navel, gently let your legs relax to the floor, allowing your feet to fall gently apart as you do so. Your arms should also relax into the ground, letting your hands rest lightly with their backs making contact with the floor.
- Bring your attention to your head and face. Beginning right at the top of your head, imagine that you are relaxing the muscles of your scalp, letting go of any tension that is held there. Move down your forehead and face in the same way, again observing any tightness that you feel there and consciously letting it go.
- As you relax your face, concentrate on any area which you feel is holding a lot of tension. Feel the softness and relaxation enter your eyes, nose, cheeks, lips, jaw and throat. You may find that your lips part gently as your face relaxes: this is a good sign that suggests you are achieving full relaxation.

- Carry on this process for each area of your body in turn, moving in sequence from your neck to the shoulders, arms, hands, the chest, abdomen, buttocks, thighs, knees, ankles and feet. If you locate any areas that feel especially tight and resistant to relaxation, spend extra time on these until they feel fully softened and loosened up.
- At the end of this process you should feel fully relaxed and comfortable. Bring your attention once more to your breathing pattern, without affecting what is happening to it, and you should find that it has slowed down and regulated itself of its own accord.
- As you observe the breath, visualise energy filling your body in the form of a bright light as you breathe in, and toxic waste and negative thoughts leaving your body as you breathe out. Choose whatever images are attractive or appropriate to you: these may change as your moods fluctuate from day to day.
- Continue to breathe in this way, luxuriating in the sense of deepening relaxation for as long as you need or want to continue.
- When you are ready to end your relaxation experience, gradually bring your attention back to your surroundings. Move your hands and feet gently, stretching and flexing them in turn. Once you are ready, start to stretch your whole body, comparing how each area feels in relation to the way it felt before the relaxation exercise began.
- Finally, open your eyes slowly. Avoid sitting up too quickly, but roll gently on to your side, moving gradually into a sitting position.

This is just one simple exercise in relaxation. Remember that there are plenty of variations available on audio or video tape. It's always a good idea to experiment with a variety of different approaches until you find one that suits you. Just as exercise activities must be tailored to our individual personalities and tastes for the best results, so the same rule applies to relaxation techniques.

Remember also that you don't have to have the luxury of endless time available in order to relax. Just as exercise can be fitted into a daily routine, it's also possible to make time to do things that are relaxing. Use your imagination and follow your instincts; after all, advice and guidance can only take you so far – only you can know what feels good to you.

Confronting our demons: adopting positive thought patterns

Without even realising it, many of us are held back from achieving our maximum potential for success, creativity and fulfilment by negative thought patterns. This is because negative ways of looking at a situation can become second nature to us, rather in the same way that poor posture can feel more comfortable and natural to us than a well-balanced and aligned carriage. There is also the subtly self-fulfilling nature of a pessimistic perspective on life: if we expect very little to go right for us in life, we can unwittingly convince others that this is true. As a result, they will often overlook us when opportunities come for professional advancement or inclusion in social events. So why be surprised that we don't get the promotion for which we are perfectly well qualified, or aren't asked to the big party that we know is being planned? All these disappointments do is further convince us that we aren't successful or popular.

Ghastly as this sounds, there is a positive aspect to coming to terms with a negative perspective once we recognise that we have a problem. As soon as this happens, we are empowered to make the necessary positive changes we need to transform our lives slowly and steadily. After all, hope is only lost when we can't see that we have a problem and keep on blaming others for the things that don't go as we would wish in life.

A variety of negative emotions can have an adverse effect on how we perceive the world around us; the following are the most common drainers of confidence and positive energy that we can experience.

139

Fear

Unreasonable fear can hold us back from enjoying our lives to the
full. After all, if we are afraid to leave the house, travel on holiday, or
feel phobic about eating out in restaurants, just think of the whole
range of pleasures to which we are saying 'no'. We can also be
hampered by subtler fears that undermine our experience of life in a
more insidious way. For example, if we lack confidence at parties,
feel petrified when speaking in public, or dread the prospect of
getting older, we can feel disproportionately stressed-out when we
are reminded of these situations. On the other hand, coming to terms
with these fears can be an immensely liberating and exciting experience.

Understanding fear
When we experience fear in response to a dangerous situation, it
can save our lives by giving us the kick-start of adrenalin needed to
get us out of the threatening situation. If we didn't feel fear we
would be in greater danger, because our responses would probably
not be swift enough to get us free of whatever is threatening us. The
'flight or fight' response that occurs within the context of a dangerous
situation is appropriate and helpful. However, for many of us who
suffer from recurrent feelings of dread and fear outside an immediately threatening situation that puts us on the spot, the on-going
stress responses we experience become inappropriate to our situation
and may actually harm us.

The fear of anticipation
How many of us have heard the phrase 'there is nothing to fear but
fear itself'? Trite as it may sound, those who have suffered from
anticipatory fear linked to a specific event will have found that it is
absolutely true. In other words, imagining the fear-inducing experience with a negative perspective is usually much more frightening
and traumatic than coping with the event itself. Once we are faced
with a stressful situation, our adrenalin levels rise to help us meet

the challenge and we find that we cope much better than we could possibly have imagined. If things don't go as well as we would have liked, we can benefit from the positive aspect of learning how to handle a similar situation even better in the future.

On the other hand, if we suffer from a long-term sense of unfocused fear that is free-floating rather than being associated with a specific issue or event, we are likely to suffer from the adverse effects of the protracted secretion of adrenalin into our systems. The unfortunate problems that follow can include high blood pressure, sleep problems and a host of stress-related illnesses including migraines, digestive problems, palpitations and muscle tension. This form of on-going fear can leave us constantly fluctuating between feelings of edginess and exhaustion. Worse, we may experience feelings of blind panic that surface alarmingly in response to minor triggers that do not merit such an overboard reaction. When we have no reasonable explanation for feeling this way, even more panic is created, of course, and an unease that can make the underlying sense of fear even worse.

The roots of fear

For many of us, the origins of our problems lie in our upbringing, which is why we may have difficulty in explaining why we are reacting to a situation in a fearful way. In other words, even though we are fully grown adults, we react to threatening situations as a child would. Unfortunately, our parents create some of our fears when they try to discipline us by conjuring up fearful images. How many of us were told as children that something terrible would happen (the bogey man would get us) if we didn't behave? Suggestions like this, made repeatedly when we are very young, can create a deep-seated feeling that the world is a threatening, dangerous place where we will be at risk if we put a foot out of line.

Sadly, fear is also something that can be communicated instinctively to a young child from an anxious parent. If a parent experiences the world as a frightening place, there is every chance that this belief will be handed on to their child unless they take deliberate action to prevent it. We can end up carrying this insecurity with us through our lives, unless we acknowledge that a problem exists and can then be helped to overcome it.

Traumatic experiences that happen to us at a very young or impressionable age can also leave scars on our minds that make us fearful in later years. Experiencing a serious accident, bereavement, sexual abuse, or witnessing a violent act are just some of the experiences that can make us anxious and insecure as adults.

Coming to terms with fear

- Although our instincts may discourage us from confronting situations that make us nervous, persistently avoiding challenging experiences can make the fear even stronger and much harder to deal with in the long run. It is generally much more constructive to try and build up our confidence by confronting fearful situations in small steps with which we feel we can cope. By approaching the problem in this way, we shall probably feel less overwhelmed by the challenge we need to face. For example, if the prospect of speaking in public is terrifying, but it is something that needs to be mastered if promotion prospects are to be fulfilled, we would be foolish to try to face a large audience for our first attempt. On the other hand, if we start to build our confidence by doing small-scale presentations on a regular basis, we shall probably be able to build up slowly to more formal public speaking situations. We may never get to love being the centre of attention, but as we gain confidence in a previously frightening situation we are likely to feel much better about ourselves.
- If we suffer from specific phobias that are limiting our lives, we may benefit from professional help that is designed to help us overcome unreasonable fears. Such behavioural therapy works by slowly exposing us to the focus of our phobia in a controlled setting. By analysing our responses with the support of a psychotherapist, we are able to reprogramme our irrational feelings. Relaxation techniques such as diaphragmatic breathing and meditation may also be of use.
- Those who are more generally anxious and lacking in confidence can benefit greatly from reading some of the self-help books

currently available on the subject of understanding our fears. A list is given in the 'Further Reading' section at the back of this book.

- Positive visualisation techniques can also help to dispel our anxious feelings. When imagining a situation in which we are likely to feel threatened and fearful, it can be very therapeutic to picture ourselves involved in this activity with everything happening exactly as we would wish. We can effectively prepare ourselves for the use of visualisation techniques by doing the relaxation exercise described above in 'Relaxation and Meditation Techniques', p. 136.
- If fearful feelings have been ingrained in us from childhood, we may benefit from working with a cognitive therapist who can show us how to identify negative patterns and break free from them by adopting a more positive perspective.
- If you experience limited, anticipatory fear of a coming stressful event, see the suggestions made in the 'Anxiety' section of Chapter Six, p. 149. These should help you feel more in control when panicky, anxious feelings descend.

Guilt

There is nothing quite so inclined to sap us of vitality and sparkle than guilt, and yet it is one of the killer emotions to which we are especially susceptible. As always, we may have had guilt instilled in us at an early age, with the sad result that we may never feel that what we achieve as adults is good enough. Once we have fallen into this trap of negative thinking, we may metaphorically beat ourselves around the head constantly for not being responsible, caring, successful, or attractive enough. The end result is that we may take refuge in comfort eating or destructive behaviour patterns which only make us feel worse in the long run by causing more guilt.

Understanding guilt

If this strikes a familiar chord, it can be immensely helpful to consider how the roots of our tendency to feel unnecessarily guilty lie in the past. How did our parents, close friends or lovers treat us? Have we felt valued, special and gifted – or unappreciated and overlooked? Sadly, if we have not felt loved for ourselves as individuals, there is a strong chance that we feel bound to strive for perfection in order to qualify for the loving we crave. Of course, perfection isn't possible, so we are bound to fall short of our own expectations and experience painful feelings of guilt and inadequacy.

Unfortunately, guilty people often attract manipulative characters like a magnet, so that their problems get more deeply ingrained and harder to handle. Many of us who experienced emotional blackmail and subtle manipulation in childhood from parents, brothers, sisters, friends or close relatives may unconsciously continue to play the same role in relation to colleagues, bosses or lovers.

Breaking free of this vicious circle can be difficult at first, because we may be trying to liberate ourselves from emotional patterns that have become second nature to us. Learning new ways of looking at ourselves and others can be very painful at first, but once we get used to the novelty of challenging long-held negative preconceptions of ourselves, we are unlikely to want to go back to old habits.

Coming to terms with guilt

- Next time feelings of guilt descend, evaluate for yourself just how justified they are. One of the most important ways of achieving a balanced perspective is to look as realistically as possible at the course of action you have taken. The chances are that you have done your best within the limitations of the situation. You may come to realise that you could have acted differently and will benefit from this insight when confronted with a similar situation in the future. On the other hand, it is also important that we appreciate the positive aspects of our actions rather than always be too hard on ourselves.

- If feelings of guilt centre around a particular issue or individual, while other areas of life feel more balanced and healthily guilt-free, it can be helpful to examine the guilt-inducing situation more carefully. We may then find that either we can actually do a bit more to improve the situation, or that we are doing our maximum and the power to move the situation in a positive direction is not within our gift. If we find the latter is the case, we may eventually reach a decision to avoid people or situations which induce negative or unjustified guilt in order to stay positive ourselves.

- We need to build our confidence by celebrating our positive aspects. If someone pays us a compliment, make a point of appreciating it at face value, rather than spending time looking for a negative hidden meaning. When things are going well and we feel happy, appreciate every moment. Most of all, forget childhood warnings that laughter will soon be followed by tears: revel in the laughter instead and enjoy every minute of it.

- Above all, we should resist any guilty feelings that surface when we are having harmless fun. Everybody needs to let their hair down from time to time and just be plain silly; provided this doesn't hurt anyone, it can feel immensely therapeutic to stop being serious for a while.

- If severe or well-established feelings of guilt are seriously preventing us from enjoying a good quality of life, it may be helpful to seek professional help from a psychotherapist.

Envy

Envy, resentment and bitterness are some of the most potent self-sabotaging emotions around. At the heart of envy lies the coveting of what someone else has, whether it is their looks, success, partner, clothes, taste, house, or popularity. Genuine admiration is quite different to resentment and envy; the former can inspire us, while the latter disempowers by filling us with negative emotions. Longing for what we don't or can't have also has the unfortunate effect of preventing us from appreciating what is positive in our own lives.

Coming to terms with envy

- If you catch yourself feeling envious and resentful towards someone, look at ways in which you can improve your own situation and so boost your self-esteem. Sometimes envy can be a sign that we aren't spending enough time and energy on ourselves in order to make our lives as enjoyable and rewarding as possible. If boredom has crept up on us as a problem, we need to find ways of improving our social lives, taking up a new interest, or changing jobs. If we feel dissatisfied with our looks, we can start exercising, consider a new look by changing hairstyles, or make a radically honest evaluation of how well we eat, and revamp whatever needs urgent attention.

- When envy descends, we can try turning the situation on its head by thinking of all of the attributes that others might see in us. If we focus often and long enough on the positive aspects of ourselves, we may come to appreciate that we all have strengths and weaknesses; too often we see the positive in others while persistently ignoring it in ourselves.

- If you feel that you are increasingly being eaten up by bitterness because you are having trouble coming to terms with past mistakes, you should consider seeking professional help in the form of counselling. This is especially worth pursuing if feelings of resentment and unhappiness are mixed up with unresolved grief, anxiety or depression.

Anger

Anger in itself, unlike envy, need not be a negative emotion. On the contrary, feeling justifiable anger in an unfair situation and expressing it in an appropriate way can be an extremely empowering and liberating experience. On the other hand, repressing anger on a regular basis can have a negative impact on our personalities, making us feel resentful and even depressed if these emotions are kept submerged for too long.

If we find ourselves constantly and unfairly bickering with those around us, the chances are that we are overlooking a more profound anger that has not been expressed in the past. If this seems to be the case, it can be helpful to pause for a moment before flying off the handle and examine how we really feel at that moment. There is a good chance that we shall recognise that we are over-reacting to the immediate situation; we may even gain some insight into the dynamics that are fuelling our anger. If this happens, we may have the chance of expressing justified anger in an assertive way to the person who is responsible.

For basic advice on how to become assertive rather than angry and aggressive in an emotionally difficult situation, see the 'First steps in assertiveness' on p. 31. As always, if anger is dominating our lives in a negative way, we should seek professional help in the form of counselling or psychotherapy.

6

Quick-fix Boosters or Rapid Rescue Techniques

By this stage of following the six-point plan you should find that general problems of fatigue, lack of 'get up and go' and recurrent major infections are largely a thing of the past.

However, life has a tendency to throw the unexpected at us at the least predictable moment, which can knock us temporarily off balance. This chapter provides a series of 'quick-fix' strategies that will help you over these acute crises in double-quick time. The six-point plan is intended to give you the basic lifestyle tools to improve your overall experience of health to the point where minor health problems remain as mere blips, or cease to occur at all. With this in mind, do not be tempted to skip the other five points of the plan and concentrate only on the quick-fix strategies as a way of managing acute health problems. Effective as these measures are, they are intended to be used on a short-term basis only.

In order to get at the root of a problem, a preventative approach is absolutely essential. This will enable us to spot the danger signals of a developing problem and take appropriate action, ideally before symptoms arise. It is precisely this sense of positive body awareness that lies at the heart of the six-point plan. Once acquired, it will become your greatest ally in achieving and maintaining high-level health.

Anxiety

Nothing is quite so draining as the symptoms of acute anxiety. Severe features of this problem include the unpleasant sensations of palpitations (consciousness of irregular or rapid heartbeat), hot flushes or clammy sweats, dry mouth, nausea, diarrhoea, muscle trembling and an overwhelming sense of fear that can result in frequent and unpredictable panic attacks.

If anxiety has become a severe or established feature it is essential to seek professional medical help in order to obtain maximum support in overcoming the problem. This advice may come from your GP, who may suggest counselling or cognitive therapy, or from appropriate alternative medical systems such as homoeopathy, medical herbalism, acupuncture or, in less acute cases, aromatherapy or reflexology.

However, if you feel generally calm and relaxed most of the time, but find that specific, infrequent situations raise your anxiety levels to an unacceptable point where they have an adverse effect on your performance, you may find the following advice invaluable in managing a short-term problem.

Identifying the triggers of anxiety

One of the most basic tools we have at our disposal in actively diffusing anxious feelings is identifying the situations that are most likely to set off these feelings in us. Problem situations may include:

- Speaking in public
- Examinations or assessments
- Social settings such as a large party
- Any professional or social setting where we feel obliged to perform in some way
- Relationship problems
- Financial crises.

Once we know the triggers that make us feel vulnerable, we are in a much stronger position to deal with the situation in a positive way. The measures that we can employ are outlined below. In addition, always bear in mind that it is not only difficult or negative circumstances that can lead us to feel anxious or on edge. In many cases, extremely exciting or positively stimulating situations can give us the nervous 'edge' that we need to perform at our best and most clear-headed. We only need to take action when we find that anticipatory anxiety is hindering us or standing in the way of our achieving desirable goals.

Taking action: immediate measures

Breathing techniques

As soon as we feel the first flutterings of anxiety, learning a relaxing way of breathing can help us diffuse feelings of panic and tension almost instantly. In order to use our breathing patterns as a way of inducing a calm and relaxed state of mind, we first need to observe how we breathe when we feel tense and anxious. All of us tend to breathe both rapidly and in a shallow way when we feel threatened; this is characterised by most of the movement coming from our upper chest. Unfortunately, however instinctive this is, it has a counterproductive effect on our state of mind, because it adversely affects the ratio of oxygen to carbon dioxide in our bodies. In order to learn a relaxed way of breathing we need to rest our hands gently on the area between the base of our rib cage and our navel. When we breathe in, we should feel our hands lifting slightly upwards and outwards as our lungs gently expand with air from the base to the tip. As a result, our upper chests should be the last area to inflate as we fill our lungs with air. Hold the breath for a second, then slowly exhale, emptying the lungs from the top first until the hands slide back into their initial position. Breathe slowly and rhythmically in this way for ten breaths to start with. If you begin to feel light-headed just breathe normally for a few seconds and then begin your relaxing breathing again once you feel ready. Although it will feel very strange at first to breathe from the diaphragm in this way, you will find in time that it gets very much easier. In addition, once you experience the direct benefits that come with this way of relaxed breathing (such as an immediate release of anxiety and greater clear-headedness), it will become a positive tool that can be used at your disposal whenever a stressful situation presents itself. Perhaps most significantly of all, it will give you a feeling of being able to take a positive step to control feelings of anxiety – something that makes a huge psychological difference when we are in a distressing situation that tends to result in great fear of loss of control. Use this tool whenever you feel the first flutterings of anxiety and it will serve you well.

Flower essences

Always carry a small bottle of Rescue Remedy with you to keep feelings of anxiety and stress at bay. The small size of this flower remedy is discreet enough to keep in a pocket or small bag. When rapid action needs to be taken, a few drops may be placed on or under the tongue (the taste is not at all unpleasant, just alcohol flavoured). As soon as you feel reassured and calm there is no need to take any more unless feelings of anxiety return. However, in situations where you have more privacy, a few drops of Rescue Remedy should be dissolved in a small glass of water or fruit juice and sipped as often as required.

Homoeopathic help

Feelings of anxiety that occur abruptly and with accompanying feelings of terror, palpitations, panic and restlessness may be considerably eased by Aconite. Because this remedy has a very rapid action and short duration you should see a marked improvement within minutes rather than hours.

However, if anxiety is generally sparked off by anticipating a specifically stressful or demanding event, it would be more appropriate to consider the homoeopathic remedies Arg nit or Gelsemium. If Arg nit is needed, feelings of anxiety are accompanied by an uncontrollable need to chatter, cravings for stimulants such as sugary foods and drinks, and 'nervous' digestive upsets such as nausea and diarrhoea. On the other hand, anticipatory anxiety that leads to withdrawal from company, brooding on stressful events, light-headedness, tension headaches, and trembling would suggest that a few doses of Gelsemium would be more appropriate.

Long-term action

Nutritional approaches
Certain foods and drinks can make us feel jittery and anxious and are best avoided, especially at times of stress. These include coffee, strong tea, sugary items such as biscuits, cakes, sweet drinks, alcohol and chocolate. Ironically, these are the very foods that we often crave when we are feeling under pressure, due to the brief 'lift' that they provide. Sadly, this sense of comfort is rapidly followed by a return to feeling tense, jittery and exhausted.

However, the good news is that there are effective substitutes that we can introduce into our diet so that we do not end up feeling deprived as well as anxious. These include herbal teas such as fennel and camomile, or fruit flavours such as raspberry, coffee substitutes made from grains such as barley, decaffeinated coffee (look for varieties where the caffeine has been removed by a water-filtering process rather than those that have been subjected to chemical solvents), non-alcoholic sparkling drinks based on herbal and fruit ingredients, regular portions of fresh fruit and vegetables, and wholemeal products (which are rich in B vitamins which play a positive role in maintaining the health of the nervous system).

If jitteriness and light-headedness are frequent problems, it is worth considering your eating patterns in an average day. If you have a tendency to go for a few hours without eating, or rely on a frequent coffee and sugary snack to keep you going in between meals, there is a good chance that your blood sugar levels are unstable. This can lead to a problem with low blood sugar (hypoglaecemia) which can be easily rectified by eating small amounts every two hours. Ideally, go for fruit, bite-sized pieces of raw vegetables, or rice cakes with savoury toppings which will stabilise blood sugar levels, rather than biscuits or chocolate which can have a counterproductive effect.

Herbal infusions

If you are going through an anxious or tense time, make a point of taking a soothing herbal infusion on a regular basis. Relaxing herbs include camomile, limeflower and valerian. However, it is important to remember that valerian should not be taken routinely over an extended period of time or in large amounts, since it can, paradoxically, promote symptoms of headaches, palpitations and muscle spasms. The best way of avoiding this problem is to rotate your choice of herbal infusion so that a single herb is not taken too frequently.

Aromatherapy oils

An anxiety-diffusing, relaxing bath may be enjoyed by adding five or six drops of any of the following essential oils to a warm bath: bergamot, clary sage, lavender, or ylang-ylang. Always remember to add the oils very sparingly after the bathwater has finished running, otherwise there is a risk that the oils will evaporate rapidly if added while the hot water is running into the bath.

Adding two or three drops of any of the following essential oils to every five mls of carrier oil provides us with a soothing and relaxing massage oil that can help us when we feel on edge: geranium, bergamot, camomile and clary sage.

Exercise to the rescue

If you suffer from muscular tension as a result of persistent anxiety you can reap huge benefits from taking regular exercise. When we are physically active we give our bodies a vital opportunity of burning up the excess adrenalin that is inevitably produced when we register feelings of anxiety and fear. If we have an excessive amount of adrenalin circulating in our bodies on a long-term basis we are likely to experience problems with raised blood pressure, poor sleep patterns and disorders of the digestive system.

On the other hand, enjoying physical exercise when we feel anxious and tense gives us a much needed chance to burn off an excess of adrenalin, with the result that we should feel more physically and mentally relaxed as a result. Choose any form of physical activity that is appealing to you, avoiding anything that feels boring or tedious, otherwise it will be given up very quickly. One of the golden rules of exercising is to aim for regularity rather than length of time spent in physical activity. In other words, it is more beneficial to spend twenty minutes exercising three times each week, rather than a single punishing two or three hour session every couple of weeks.

Burn out

Living in the pressured way that we do, it should come as little surprise that stress-related problems are one of the major causes of time spent off work. These problems could also be regarded as a significant threat to the quality of life that we generally experience. Although a variety of stress-related conditions are discussed in specific sections of this chapter (insomnia, anxiety and fatigue), the state of 'burn out' described in this section may be regarded as a general fundamental response to an overly-stressed lifestyle.

Experiencing burn out usually involves a range of symptoms and sensations that affect us physically, mentally and emotionally. These may include unstable and undependable energy levels, physical weakness and lack of stamina, lack of concentration, mood swings and lowered levels of confidence.

If these symptoms have become part of a recurrent or persistent pattern, or if they seem to be a fundamental part of your physical and emotional make-up, this would suggest that professional help is required to deal with the problem at a fundamental level. Psychological techniques such as cognitive therapy can be of great help in such situations, encouraging us to see how we may unconsciously sabotage ourselves by adopting destructive lifestyle patterns. When cognitive therapy is employed effectively, it gives us the mental tools we need to change our destructive patterns and replace them with a positive response.

We may also be helped by alternative medical therapies that concentrate on stimulating our energy levels, such as traditional Chinese medicine, homoeopathy, shiatsu or acupressure. As always, if problems are well-established it is best to seek treatment from a trained practitioner rather than attempting to deal with the situation by self-help measures alone.

On the other hand, if you generally find that you function very effectively, but that a period of unusual physical, mental or emotional strain has left you feeling depleted, following the advice given below may be enough to get you back on track.

Identifying the triggers of burn out

Any of the following situations may result in our feeling substantially depleted of mental, emotional and physical energy:

- A temporarily extra-stressful situation at work involving extra responsibility, longer working hours and a general atmosphere of stress among colleagues
- Losing sleep over a significant period of time
- Nursing a sick relative both day and night
- Long-term emotional or financial problems for which a solution seems elusive

- A severe viral infection with not enough time available to convalesce in an adequate way
- Too much exposure to people and situations that are emotionally demanding and draining
- Adopting an unrealistic exercise regime after months or years of physical inactivity.

Taking action: immediate measures

Work strategies

If you find that you are especially stressed at work in order to meet a short-term deadline, make sure that you have a proper lunch break rather than giving in to pressure to work through this important time off. This is not only essential time for relaxation, but it is also vitally important as a way of maintaining smooth and easy digestion. If we slip into the common habit of grabbing a snack while we sit at our desks, there is a strong risk that we shall end up with indigestion, heartburn and a generally uncomfortable digestive system.

Learn to say 'no' firmly and politely when you know you have reached your maximum work load. We all have different levels of capacity for immersion in work, but we also usually have an instinctive sense of when we are sufficiently stretched and challenged by our work to perform well. This is the level you need to aim for most of the time, with only brief periods of being pushed a little harder. If we begin to tolerate work patterns that persistently tax us beyond a productive and stimulating level, we are inevitably heading for a state of burn out. This does not mean that we need to seem unenthusiastic about our work, merely that we recognise the boundaries within which we are able to perform at our productive best.

Homoeopathic help

A general state of physical burn out that is the result of taking on board an unrealistic amount of exercise after years of being physically inactive may benefit considerably from a few doses of Arnica.

Symptoms that are greatly relieved by taking this remedy include a general feeling of soreness, aching and tenderness throughout the body, coupled with an overwhelming feeling of tiredness and exhaustion with muscle strain.

On the other hand, if burn out occurs as result of 'burning the candle at both ends', with a tendency to rely on stimulants such as tea and coffee to keep going and/or alcohol and cigarettes in order to relax, we are likely to see rapid benefit from the homoeopathic remedy Nux vomica. Short-term choice of this remedy would be confirmed if symptoms of sleep disturbance, muscle tension and mental exhaustion are marked. Using Nux vomica in a stressful situation on a short-term basis when the symptoms are appropriate can give us the energy kick-start needed to free ourselves from rushing to chemical stimulants and relaxants in order to cope.

Aromatherapy oils
Mental fatigue and temporary muzzy-headedness may be rapidly eased by placing one or two drops of the following essential oils on a tissue or handkerchief and inhaling as often as required. Appropriate oils include: lavender, grapefruit, eucalyptus,* rosemary and peppermint.* (Oils marked with a * may interfere with the action of homoeopathic remedies.)

Long-term action

Relaxation techniques
One of the fundamental ways of avoiding burn out is to make relaxation techniques or meditation a basic part of your life. Luckily, there are increasingly large numbers of tapes on the market that take us through a guided relaxation exercise. There is also a burgeoning market for Yoga video tapes, which will usually include a basic relaxation section or show us very basic ways to meditate. Once these skills have been mastered, get into the habit of spending a short time each day consciously relaxing mentally and developing an awareness of the tension-holding areas in our bodies. As we get

used to the sensations of physical and mental relaxation, the tension is encouraged to melt away from tight or strained areas. This has the dual effect of giving us a realisation of how it feels to be deeply relaxed, and also the essential bonus of putting us in touch with our bodies.

Exercise techniques

It is worth enrolling in a Yoga or T'ai chi course in order to learn a form of body movement that is rather like meditation in action. Both forms of exercise emphasise the importance of breathing techniques, while also increasing physical flexibility, strength and stamina. Perhaps most importantly, these forms of movement are non-competitive in nature, so that marked emphasis is put on always being aware of how far our bodies will go, and never forcing or pushing these boundaries too far. Because of this gentle but dynamic approach, physical injury as a result of stress or trauma is unlikely to occur, while a basic sense of relaxation should be increased. Do not be misled into thinking that these are soft options for those who want a substitute for 'real', punishing exercise techniques. On the contrary, the practice of Yoga and T'ai chi will boost our levels of muscular co-ordination, suppleness and strength.

Nutritional approaches

Although it may sound contradictory advice, it is best to avoid foods that give us a 'quick fix' when we feel stressed and need a burst of energy. These foods and drinks are quite easily identified, because they usually fall into the category of junk or convenience foods and include any of the following items: crisps, nuts, chocolate, coffee, tea, hot chocolate, 'instant' noodles or soups, biscuits, cakes and any other items made from a high proportion of white flour, white sugar, and fat (which is usually hydrogenated and, as a result, harmful to us). Far from giving us increased, sustained levels of physical and mental energy, these foods quickly lead to a rapid slump in energy after a short-lived boost. We are likely to respond to this dip in energy by taking more of the sweet or junk food in order to recapture that elusive 'lift'. Once this becomes an established pattern of eating, we shall experience persistently unpredictable and lowered levels of energy, with associated instability of mood, lowered levels of concentration and irritability. In order to avoid this vicious cycle, we should try to concentrate instead on including items in the diet that provide us with more sustained and constant levels of energy. These would include whole grains such as wholemeal bread, frequent portions of fresh fruit and vegetables, pulses, unroasted nuts and seeds, and small amounts of fish and poultry. Coffee, strong tea, and alcohol should only be taken in moderation, keeping coffee and alcohol well within recommended daily intake (less than two cups of coffee a day and less than two units of alcohol, a unit being one small glass of wine or half a pint of beer).

Exercise addiction and physical burn out

If we have taken up a sporting activity and are fiercely competitive by nature, or if we have become heavily involved in a punishing exercise regime in order to compensate for a poor body image or low self-esteem, there is a strong chance that we may be at risk of experiencing physical burn out. This need not happen if we enjoy taking regular exercise within the context of a well-balanced and satisfying domestic, social and professional life. On the contrary, this type of exercise can provide a very positive sense of physical and mental release and improve our overall experience of living. Danger signs of exercise addiction occur when keeping up with a punishing exercise schedule becomes more important than keeping up a lively social life, or relaxing with family members. If any danger signs are spotted, it is important to seek professional advice in order to help us come to terms with the underlying emotional tensions and conflicts that may be masked by an undue attachment to exercise.

Herbal-scented baths

Make a point of regularly making an infusion of relaxing herbs (rosemary or peppermint) that can be added to your bathwater for a soothing soak whenever mental, emotional and physical energy levels appear to be flagging. Make a strong infusion by adding three generous handfuls of dried herb to a medium-sized pan of cold water and leaving it to steep overnight. Bring the infusion to the boil the following morning and strain. Store the clarified infusion in a screw-top jar in a cool place and add whenever required to a warm bath.

Insomnia

The world appears to be divided between those who can sleep at the drop of a hat, and those who barely know what it is to have a sound or refreshing night's rest. However, even those of us who normally sleep quite easily can find that we experience short-term insomnia as a result of being under an unusual amount of stress, eating and/or drinking unwisely, or after travelling on a long-haul flight.

As with any well-established health problem, a tendency to severe sleep disruption should be treated by a health professional. Bear in mind that if you are unhappy about using conventional sleeping tablets because of their possible tendency to promote dependence or rebound insomnia, there is a substantial amount of help available from an alternative medical source.

Alternative treatments to consider for the relief of chronic sleep disturbance include Western medical herbalism, homoeopathy, hypnotherapy and aromatherapy. If sleep problems are combined with a tendency to anxiety, it is also worth exploring help from a psychological perspective such as autogenic training or cognitive therapy.

On the other hand, a brief episode of poor sleep quality in response to an obvious trigger may be substantially and rapidly improved by adopting some of the self-help measures listed below.

Identifying the triggers of insomnia

Any of the following common factors can affect our sleep pattern in an adverse way if they continue for too long:

- Too much caffeine in the diet from an excess of strong tea, coffee, chocolate, or fizzy drinks
- Working too late and too intensely
- Not having enough time to relax and unwind
- A working framework that involves irregular hours or a large amount of time travelling
- Eating heavy meals too late at night
- Too little physical activity or exposure to fresh air during the day
- Caring for a small baby or sick relative at night
- Coping with a period of severe or extended stress
- Certain specific medical conditions which can lead to sleep problems, such as pre-menstrual syndrome, the menopause, depression, or anxiety.

Taking action: immediate measures

Herbal help

Relaxing herbs can be used in a variety of ways to help ensure that we get a sound night's sleep. At the first sign of sleeplessness, try valerian tablets to see if they can re-establish a healthy sleep pattern. In addition, a strong infusion of sleep-promoting herbs can be added to your bath water in order to prepare you before retiring: these may include lavender, camomile, or limeflower.

Aromatherapy oils

Any of the following essential oils may be used sparingly to induce a sound sleep. One or two drops can be burnt in a custom-made diffuser by the bedside, or dropped on the pillow. Appropriate oils include camomile, lavender, or ylang-ylang.

Alternatively, a soothing bath can be enjoyed by adding five or six drops of essential oil to a warm bath once the taps have stopped running. However, make sure that the bath water is not too hot, since this can have an adverse effect by preventing, rather than inducing, sleep. It is also likely to make the essential oils evaporate too quickly, thus reducing their potential relaxing effect.

Green magic

Taking a cup of lettuce tea before bed is reputed to aid relaxation and contribute to a sound and refreshing sleep. This simple tea can be made by adding a generous helping of fresh, chopped lettuce leaves to a cup and a half of boiling water. Leave to infuse for a few minutes before straining off the liquid and sipping as a relaxing bedtime drink.

Homoeopathic help

Temporary insomnia that arises from short-term anxiety about meeting high standards at work may benefit from a few doses of Arsenicum album. Choice of this remedy would be confirmed by a tendency to wake after midnight, especially if sleeplessness is accompanied by marked chilliness and restlessness. Additional symptoms that would point to the choice of this remedy include a general desire for warmth, with great comfort being obtained from frequent sips of a warm drink.

On the other hand, short-term insomnia that follows the shock of bad news or an accident may respond better to Aconite. Symptoms that would suggest this approach is needed include a severe state of restlessness with constant tossing and turning in the bed in an attempt to get comfortable. Once asleep, nightmares are common, with the likelihood of waking with severe anxiety or sensations of panic.

Brief but severely disrupted sleep quality that occurs as a result of working extra-long hours in order to meet an unusually tight dead-line is more likely to be swiftly rectified by a few doses of Nux vomica. This is an especially appropriate remedy to choose if there is a tendency to rely on strong tea and coffee as stimulants in order to keep working abnormally long hours, with resulting difficulty in switching off once in bed. If alcohol consumption has also temporarily increased as an additional support for switching off, with attendant morning-after headaches, choice of this remedy would be confirmed.

Warm footbaths
If you feel tense before retiring and want a quick way of winding down, try relaxing for a few minutes with your feet soaking in warm water. For an extra-soothing effect, add a strong infusion of camomile tea to the water.

Long-term action

Lifestyle
There are certain practical considerations that we should not overlook if sleep problems are beginning to affect our lives. Above all else, we should make sure that our bedrooms include the basic elements conducive to a good night's sleep. These include a room that is neither too hot nor too cold; enough darkness to ensure rest (but not so much that it gets difficult to wake in the morning); and sufficient sound-proofing to filter out loud noises such as the movement of traffic in the early hours of the morning.

Nutritional approaches
If sleep quality has been gradually declining, check your diet in order to make sure that you have not gradually been increasing the amount of coffee, tea, chocolate or caffeinated fizzy drinks that you take. It is possible for the amount to build up insidiously without our noticing it, especially if we are experiencing extra stress. If you are surprised by your overall consumption, do not be tempted to cut out all sources of caffeine as a desperate measure, since this can trigger unpleasant symptoms of caffeine withdrawal. Instead, reduce the number of caffeinated drinks slowly and steadily, systematically increasing the amount of decaffeinated drinks and herbal teas that you drink.

Always make a point of not eating a heavy meal before bed, because we are less able to sleep well if our stomachs are busily at work trying to digest a large meal. Because our bodies need to go into resting mode overnight, putting an unwanted burden on the digestive system at an inappropriate time is totally counter-productive. All we are likely to end up with is an unfortunate combination of restless sleep and indigestion.

Essential exercise

If you have a history of poor sleep patterns, it can be immensely helpful to make sure that you take regular aerobic exercise three, or ideally four, times a week. It is also important to try to enjoy your aerobic activities out of doors so that you have the maximum exposure to fresh air, which can be an important co-factor in inducing a sound night's rest. Make a point of choosing activities that you enjoy, so that you are far more likely to keep up the routine. Always remember that boredom is one of the greatest disincentives to keeping up the habit of exercise.

Relaxation strategies

Make a positive point of relaxing and unwinding for at least an hour before it is time to go to bed. Above all, avoid the temptation to squeeze in some extra mental work just before it is time to go to sleep. By giving in to this temptation we make it more difficult for our minds to switch off and relax, since they are still likely to be working in problem-solving mode at the very time they need to be preparing themselves for relaxation.

Instead of mulling through problems in your head before sleep, try listening to a soothing piece of music, playing a relaxation tape, sipping a warm drink, or reading a novel.

Recurrent infections

All of us are likely to experience the odd cold or sore throat at some time or another, and this need not signify anything sinister at all. In fact, some sources suggest that experiencing the very occasional minor cold may give our bodies a positive opportunity for a 'spring clean', as mucous discharges flush away the by-products of infection.

On the other hand, if we find ourselves in a downward spiral of constant minor infections affecting the throat and chest, we may begin to feel that we are never completely free of coughs and colds. In this situation we may even begin to feel that we are experiencing one permanent cold, since we are unable to identify where one illness ends and the other begins.

This is definitely a situation that calls for swift and positive action, since it suggests that we are in a physically run-down state that is leaving us unable to fight off infection effectively. In order to deal with the problem, we need to concentrate on ways of boosting our immune system to fight illness efficiently, as well as adopting a variety of alternative medical measures that can support us through the acute phase of a cold as swiftly as possible, leaving us less prone to the risk of complications such as ear or chest infections.

Identifying the triggers of recurrent infection

It is a striking fact that even though a nasty, highly-infectious cold may be doing the rounds, not everyone catches it. In fact, we may already have identified those friends and colleagues who seem to be maddeningly immune to sniffles and sore throats, while we seem to succumb to infection at the drop of a hat.

The key to this mystery lies in the concept of susceptibility. In other words, if we take a sample of people who are all exposed to the same bacterial or viral infection at the same time, it will be noticeable that some of these people repeatedly develop an infectious illness while others have only minimal symptoms or develop nothing at all. As a result of this experience, we need to pay attention to those who fight infection vigorously and well so that we can encourage our bodies to do the same.

Some of us may inherit strong constitutions and efficient immune systems; others of us may have learnt the hard way that our bodies need basic maintenance and positive support in order to do their best for us. Conversely, we are also likely to have learnt about the factors that lead our immune systems to let us down. These factors may include any of the following:

- A consistently poor diet that denies our bodies the basic building blocks needed to maintain our systems in peak condition
- Lack of good quality, refreshing sleep for a protracted period of time
- Working conditions that include open plan offices, poorly-functioning air conditioning and central heating systems
- Coping with protracted stress without being able to put stress-reducing strategies in place
- An inability to relax and unwind.

Taking action: immediate measures

Vitamin C to the rescue

Taking a vitamin C supplement at the first sign of a cold developing can do a great deal to limit the duration of infection and discourage the possibility of further complications. Although there has been some recent controversy about the safety of using this vitamin supplement, the current informed opinion seems to be that it presents an unlikely source of toxic problems. On the contrary, it appears to be more likely to have a beneficial effect by supporting our immune systems in fighting infection. If you are working closely with colleagues who are coughing and sneezing all around you, consider taking 500 milligrams (half a gram) a day for the duration of the period you are actively exposed to infection. On the other hand, if you have already developed early symptoms of a cold, it would be more appropriate to consider using one or two grams of vitamin C a day, ideally in slow-release form so that you get a steady supply during a twenty-four hour period. This is especially relevant when taking doses of vitamin C, because it tends to stay in the body a relatively short time (roughly four hours) before it is excreted. As a result, it is rather wasteful to take your two grams in one dose. Continue with this regime while cold symptoms persist, reducing the amount taken if any symptoms of acidity in the stomach or loose stools arise.

Rest cures

Although we may find ourselves under a huge amount of pressure to continue working through a severe infectious illness such as a heavy cold, it is very important to resist this approach. Taking a few days off at the infectious stage of illness can make a significant difference on a purely practical level: it prevents the spread of infection to colleagues who are bound to pass it on to others. Resting at home also frees up energy that is tremendously important in fighting infection; if we use it up by working when we already feel washed-out, there is every chance that the infection will continue for a longer period than necessary. It also increases the possibility of relapse or secondary complications.

Try to keep in as consistent a temperature as possible, since adjusting to movement from one temperature to another also uses up energy reserves that are best kept for fighting illness efficiently.

Humidifying techniques

If your nasal passages feel inflamed and blocked, use a humidifier, or place bowls of cold water near each radiator to humidify the atmosphere naturally. Two or three drops of any of the following essential oils may be added to a steam inhalation in order to clear stuffy nasal passages: lavender, tea tree, peppermint,* or eucalyptus.* (Essential oils marked with a * may interfere with the medicinal action of homoeopathic remedies.)

De-tox

Keep fluid intake high in order to flush toxins out of the body as efficiently as possible and reduce the risk of feverishness developing. Although a fever can be helpful in 'burning out' the infection, a very high temperature can be difficult to manage if you are looking after yourself, and can feel extremely debilitating. There is also a good chance that your appetite will be reduced while infection is at its height, which makes it absolutely essential that fluid intake is more than adequate. Choose mineral water, herb teas and fruit juices, avoiding milky drinks (which can make mucous congestion worse) or tea and coffee (which act as diuretics, increasing the amount of liquid that is excreted from the body).

Nutritional approaches

Food should be light, appetising and as nutritious as possible. Avoid heavy or fatty items that take a long time to digest and use up energy needed for fighting infection. Opt instead for fresh fruit and vegetables that will boost your intake of vitamin C, and easily-digested soups and purees.

Soothing teas and gargles

Sore throats may be soothed by sipping warm infusions of water with a dash of lemon and a teaspoonful of honey. A simple gargle may also be made by dissolving a teaspoonful of salt and vinegar in a cup of warm water. However, make sure that the mixture isn't accidentally swallowed, because it may make you sick.

An infusion of basil with a pinch of cloves taken in the early stage of a cold makes a pleasant-tasting tea that feels comforting as well as encouraging a mild sweat.

Herbal help

Echinacea may be taken in liquid or tablet form to help the body in fighting infection. It should be taken as soon as symptoms appear, and may be continued as long as symptoms persist. Although some sources suggest that it can be taken as a general immune-system booster over the winter, other sources claim that echinacea has maximum impact if it is used on a short-term basis rather than routinely over an extended period.

Homoeopathic help

If symptoms of a heavy cold or flu emerge abruptly, with feverishness, severely inflamed throat and a general sensation of feeling hot, bothered and incredibly irritable, a few doses of Belladonna in homoeopathic potency should speed up recovery.

On the other hand, if general symptoms of feeling ill in a non-specific way have been around for a few days, with heavy limbs, overwhelming fatigue, headache like a tight band around the head, and chill and shivers running up and down the spine, the chances are that Gelsemium is more likely to be appropriate.

Once the initial stage of infection has passed, another remedy is likely to be called for, as a cold or flu moves on to its second phase. If the primary problem at this stage is a severe head cold, with a nose that alternates between running like a tap and being dry and stuffed up, cold sores around the mouth or nose, and severe and frequent bouts of sneezing that are much worse for bright light, the remedy Nat mur should ease symptoms considerably and shorten the duration of the problem.

Once symptoms have reached a lingering stage with the production of abundant, thick, yellowy-green mucus, an alternately dry and loose cough (often productive in the morning and dry at night), with painful sinuses in the cheeks and over the eyes, and a general sense of discomfort from being overheated, Pulsatilla should finish off the symptoms decisively and with the minimum amount of fuss.

Long-term action

The importance of sleep

We must enjoy regular periods of good quality, refreshing sleep if we are to enjoy maximum health. Not only does sleep have a profound effect on our psychological well-being and resilience, but it also plays a crucial role in maintaining the vigour and health of our immune systems. We may be able to sustain short periods of 'burning the candle at both ends' and not see any damaging consequences. However, there is every chance that once we push ourselves beyond a certain point and try to cope with too little sleep, we will soon become aware that we are not functioning at our optimum level. Initial signs of a sleep-deprived system include feeling lethargic and lacking 'get up and go'; but this can rapidly develop into a situation where one minor infection follows another, with complete recovery seeming increasingly elusive. In order to avoid this problem developing in the first place, make adequate sleeping time a priority by saying 'no' to some engagements and commitments if they interfere with your getting adequate rest. However boring this may sound as a strategy, it is well worth adopting because considerable problems can be avoided provided we get our minimum amount of quality rest.

Eating for a healthy immune system

Looking after the quality of our diet is of paramount importance if we want to enjoy maximum immune system functioning. Although it may sometimes seem inconvenient or a nuisance to make good-quality nutrition, once we realise how essential a role this plays in helping us throw off minor or recurrent infections as efficiently and quickly as possible, we are likely to put some effort into eating as well as we possibly can. Simple guidelines include making sure that we have essential anti-oxidant enzymes in our diet. These include vitamins A, C and E and the trace element selenium. Good dietary sources include fresh red and yellow fruit and vegetables, fish oils and sesame seeds. Although generally we should not rely on taking supplements in order to obtain our quota of essential vitamins and minerals, we may benefit from supplementing with anti-oxidants under special circumstances, including times of unusual stress, travelling frequently on long-haul flights and working in an office that you may suspect suffers from 'sick building syndrome'. (The latter occurs where air conditioning and/or central heating systems are not working efficiently, leading to the constant re-circulation of germs and bacteria. In addition, offices that are overloaded with

VDU screens, photocopiers and fax machines, with a lack of green plants and access to fresh air, can contribute to a negative working environment.)

The magic of garlic

Including garlic regularly in the diet can do a great deal to discourage the development of the chronic catarrhal congestion that can lead to problems such as sinusitis. Garlic is reputed to have powerful antibacterial properties (due to the presence of the active compound allicin), as well as the capacity to break down and eliminate thick or infected mucus. Increasing the amount of garlic in our daily eating regime can be a worthwhile preventive strategy in discouraging recurrent infections, but if a nasty cold has already developed, it is worth investing in a concentrated garlic supplement until infection is over. When buying a garlic supplement it is best to choose a powdered variety in coated tablet form that has a high allicin yield (the active compound that has anti-bacterial properties). It has also been suggested that our hearts and circulatory systems may benefit from taking garlic regularly.

Stomach upsets, over-indulgence and hang-overs

We are, thankfully, blissfully unaware of the functioning of our stomach and other digestive organs when all is working well. However, this can sometimes lead us to taking our stomachs for granted, and treating them with a lack of general respect for how and what we eat or drink.

Our minds can also play an important role in maintaining or subverting our overall digestive performance. A lack of ability to relax can be an important co-factor in the development of stress-related digestive disorders such as irritable bowel syndrome, or stomach ulcers. Chronic conditions such as these can benefit from general holistic treatment that focuses on the need to harmonise mind, emotions and body. Therapies that have this basic approach include homoeopathy, Western medical herbalism, traditional Chinese medicine and some nutritional therapies.

However, if your digestion is very sound as a rule, but one or more dietary mistakes have led to a temporary upset, the advice given below should sort the problem out swiftly and efficiently. Most important of all, it will also give you some basic hints to help you avoid similar problems in the future.

Identifying the triggers of stomach upsets

Any of the following can be responsible for unpleasant stomach symptoms:

- Too much alcohol, or having a disastrous mixture of different types of alcoholic drinks that do not agree with each other (such as wines and beer or lager)
- Eating a very rich meal that includes too many fatty foods or creamy sauces, accompanied with too much alcohol
- Smoking too much
- Drinking an excessive amount of strong coffee
- Not being careful enough about hygiene when preparing and cooking food.

Taking action: immediate measures

Water therapy
If the problem is clearly due to over-indulgence, it is especially important the following day to drink regular glasses of water in order to flush toxins out of the system as quickly as possible. This is of particular relevance if an overload of alcohol has been taken, since this can result in marked dehydration.

Slippery Elm solutions
If acidity and general digestive discomfort follow eating a heavy or indigestible meal, try sipping a soothing drink made from powdered

Slippery Elm bark and warm milk. Slippery Elm has a reputation for reducing irritation of the stomach lining and may be taken generally for digestive upsets.

Herbal teas

Discomfort and flatulence that follow an exciting night out may respond well to an infusion of fennel, peppermint, or lemon balm.

Spices

If you are left with queasiness or nausea the day after the night before, sucking a piece of crystallised ginger is a pleasant way of settling the stomach. Alternatively, if you are not keen on the sweetness of the crystallised variety, make a nausea-settling tea from finely-grated root ginger and warm water.

Homoeopathic help

Nausea, vomiting and diarrhoea that follow eating out may call for a few doses of Arsenicum album to settle the problem. Specific symptoms which suggest that this remedy is appropriate include distress and revulsion at the sight or smell of food, thirst for frequent small sips of water, and marked chilliness and restlessness when vomiting and diarrhoea occur together.

Classic hang-overs that involve waking with a severe headache, irritability, constipation and nausea are more likely to respond well to Nux vomica, while digestive upsets that clearly follow eating too many rich, fatty foods in one meal are more likely to clear up in response to Pulsatilla. Characteristic symptoms of the latter include a dry mouth without thirst, 'repeating' of the taste of food eaten hours earlier, and stomach pains that are much more tender after jolting or jarring movements.

Simple burping and flatulence with heavy, full sensations in the stomach should be cleared up quickly with a dose or two of Carbo veg. Choice of this remedy would be confirmed by a marked amount of bloating around the waist after eating even the smallest amount.

Long-term action

Nutritional approaches

If you have a general tendency to stomach upsets, avoid foods that can aggravate digestive discomfort. These include full fat cheeses, spicy dishes such as curries and chillies, beans, sprouts, raw onions, cabbage, red meat, strong tea, coffee and spirits. It is a good idea to include regular portions of foods that are easy on the stomach such as lightly steamed or stir-fried dishes, salads, pasta, home-made soups, small portions of chicken (eaten without the skin, which has a high percentage of fat) and fish. If your job involves regular eating out, it's a good idea to steer clear of any dishes that involve rich sauces, batters, or cream. These are not only very bad news for the waistline, but they also tend to take a long time to digest.

Try to go for small meals eaten at regular intervals rather than falling into the common habit of leaving large gaps between heavy or large meals. The latter pattern is very likely to develop without our realising it when stress levels are high and our time seems at a premium. The result is often a tendency to grab a bag of crisps, chocolate bar and a coffee while working, and a glass of wine, beer, or gin and tonic once we collapse after work in order to unwind. Before we know it, we have probably used both our recommended fat allowance and alcohol units before our evening has even begun! Try to pace yourself through the day, making time to relax while you eat your lunch and sitting down to relax for a few minutes when coming home from work, choosing a sparkling mineral water or fruit juice in preference to an extra glass of alcohol.

It is very important to avoid the temptation to rely on antacids as a way of settling an upset stomach, since a significant range of problems are associated with over-use of these over-the-counter medicines. When these products include a bicarbonate of soda base, they can cause symptoms of rebound acidity if they are used to relieve stomach upsets on a long-term basis.

The mechanism that leads to this problem is simple: when

stomach acid is diluted by an antacid there is a temporary sense of relief from discomfort and burning in the stomach. Sadly, this is only a short-lived respite because the body quickly registers that the levels of stomach acid have been considerably reduced. Its swift response is to rectify the situation by pumping more acid into the stomach in order to maintain the status quo. By the time this has happened we are effectively back to square one, with our stomachs feeling uncomfortable once again. If we are unaware of what is happening, our instinctive response is to take another antacid in order to make ourselves more comfortable. As a result, we begin to slide our way down a slippery slope where we become dependent on daily medication in order to keep symptoms at bay.

We should also be aware that there are additional problems with antacids based on bicarbonate of soda. These problems include an aggravation of high blood pressure, or water retention. Aluminium-based formulas, on the other hand, can aggravate symptoms of constipation. In addition, the controversial argument has been put forward that aluminium salts may be linked to the promotion of dementia-like symptoms. We should also be very wary of 'morning after' combination headache and stomach upset medications, since these contain painkillers that can lead to stomach bleeding. This is especially worrying if we consider that this tendency to bleeding can be increased by the presence of alcohol in the stomach.

There are certain combinations of foods that can make digestion more difficult, so if there is any sign of queasiness or digestive upset, they are best avoided. These combinations include red meat with carbohydrates such as bread or potatoes, cheese with bread, or sweet pastries with cream or custards. Try fish or chicken with steamed green vegetables or a mixed, dressed salad, and fresh fruit or sorbet to follow instead. It has been suggested that grated raw carrot, celery and pineapple have digestion-aiding qualities, as well as the spices coriander, cinnamon, cayenne and cumin.

Mood swings

All of us will experience fluctuations of mood in the course of our daily lives in response to an incredibly wide variety of triggers. These may include sleep deprivation, temporary suspension of a healthy diet, an unpleasant atmosphere at home or at work, or extra or unexpected stress. These problems should do little lasting damage to our sense of equilibrium and resilience when we are feeling good, since this is the time when our ability to cope is at its highest. This is when we are likely to deal with problems in a successful and competent way, because we are able to bring a balanced and positive perspective to them. In addition, we quickly become aware that the satisfying resolution of a difficult situation goes a long way towards making us feel even more positive and confident about ourselves.

It would be marvellous if we could enjoy this ideal every day of our lives, fulfilling our potential to the maximum without even trying. But inevitably, there are times when problems hit us at the wrong moment, or seem to pile up until we eventually feel overwhelmed by them. It is at moments like these that we can use some of the measures outlined below to get us quickly back in the driving seat again.

However, if we experience severe or extended mood swings on a regular basis, it is important to seek professional treatment. The best way to approach this problem may be an appropriate combination of orthodox and alternative therapies. This would provide an opportunity for a conventional doctor to evaluate the possible reasons for the mood swings (such as a hormone imbalance), while the appropriate alternative medical approach might provide effective treatment without the problems of potential side-effects associated with chemical drugs.

Identifying the triggers of mood swings

Coping with temporary changes of mood can be much easier to deal with once we identify the potential factors that can influence positive or negative shifts in our state of mind.

Possible mood-influencing triggers can include any of the following:

- Alcohol
- Irregular eating patterns
- Sugar
- Coffee
- Prescription drugs (such as those taken to regulate high blood pressure)
- Lack of sleep, or an excess of sleep
- Fluctuation in hormone levels (during ovulation or pre-menstrually)
- Flu (especially during or following the recovery phase)
- Stress
- Feeling socially isolated
- Lack of satisfaction at work.

Taking action: immediate measures

Blood sugar levels

If any of the following problems apply to you on a regular basis, there is a good chance that you may be suffering from hypoglycaemia (low blood sugar levels). Symptoms include mood swings, difficulty in concentrating, fluctuating energy levels and muzzy-headedness. If you recognise your symptoms in this list, try an experiment of eating every two hours, making sure that you don't skip food for a long period of time. The latter habit is often picked up unwittingly when we become immersed in a task, often forgetting how much time has gone by, especially when we are working to a pressing deadline.

Blood sugar levels may be kept more stable by choosing regular snacks of bite-sized chunks of raw vegetable, pieces of fresh fruit, wholemeal bread and salads. Avoid relying on sugary items such as cakes, biscuits or chocolate bars for a temporary energy boost.

Although these undeniably do give us a rush of increased energy, they quickly have the undesirable effect of leaving us feeling sluggish, weary and in need of another sugar boost within a short period of time. As a result, these foods contribute towards increasingly fluctuating blood sugar levels.

Beware of addictive substances

If mood swings are becoming an increasingly obvious part of your life, take a good, long, hard look at the amount of addictive items that you eat or drink within an average day. You may reject this idea out of hand because you are not an obvious candidate for cocaine or other recreational drug addiction. However, you may unwittingly be using other forms of more socially acceptable drugs in order to keep the pace. Foods, drinks and drugs that you should consider include chocolate, sugar, stimulants such as caffeine (not just in coffee or tea but also in 'hidden' sources such as fizzy drinks and natural stimulants such as gurana), painkillers that contain codeine, and alcohol.

If you take all or most of these on a daily basis, there is a fighting chance that they will contribute to moderate to marked mood swings. Although you will benefit from eliminating most of them from your diet, on no account consider kicking the habit of all of them at once. If coffee is your main addiction (and you can readily establish if it is an addiction for you by asking yourself how you would feel if you had to do without it), don't try to cut it out overnight or you may experience unpleasant symptoms of caffeine withdrawal. Instead, start to replace some of your coffee breaks with either decaffeinated coffee, grain-based coffee substitutes, or fruit teas. By reducing the amount of caffeine in your system on a steady and cumulative basis you are likely to avoid the unpleasantness of caffeine withdrawal.

On the other hand, if you couldn't care less about coffee, but find that your alcohol intake has been steadily increasing over a period of stress, evaluate realistically how much you are taking on a daily basis. If you have been taking an amount of alcohol significantly over your estimated weekly unit allowance for an extended period (fourteen units for women and twenty-one for men), you may need some professional advice and support in order to deal effectively with the problem. Otherwise, if your alcohol intake has increased slowly in the recent past and remains within the general limits of your weekly allowance, it will help your mood swings considerably to cut down on your overall alcohol consumption. Start by frequently substituting a herbal soft drink, fruit juice or mineral water for a glass of wine or measure of spirits. You needn't cut alcohol out of your diet completely, but by increasing the amount of non-alcoholic drinks that you consume you can halve the amount of alcohol that you drink in a way that shouldn't make you feel deprived. It's also a good idea to have a couple of alcohol-free nights during the week in order to give your liver a much-needed rest to recover and regenerate itself.

Once you follow these guidelines you may also be surprised to discover that you no longer need to rely on painkillers as much; a significant proportion of headaches are the result of an excessive consumption of alcohol or coffee.

Herbal help

If tension headaches occur as a result of feeling uptight and irritable, try sipping lemon verbena tea as often as required. On the other hand, camomile tea makes an excellent bedtime drink if stress and tension are contributing to difficulty in sleeping soundly.

Tincture of wild oats can be a useful ally in dealing with the tiredness and jadedness that can set in when we are trying to de-tox the system after cutting down on any of the substances mentioned above. Eight drops of the tincture may be taken, dissolved in a small glass of water each day until symptoms improve (this should happen within a few weeks and the tincture should not be taken on a routine basis after that).

Aromatherapy oils

Decant three to four drops of any of the following essential oils in a warm bath to lift and balance the mood: clary sage, lavender, ylang-ylang, or sandalwood. Let the oils float on top of the water and soak for as long as it takes to feel refreshed and uplifted.

Homoeopathic help

Temporary feelings of irritability and apathy and uncharacteristic sensations of feeling unable to cope with daily demands may clear quickly after a few doses of Sepia. This remedy is especially well-suited to mood swings that occur pre-menstrually or during the menopause.

On the other hand, mood swings that occur infrequently with poor sleep quality and a sense of feeling low on waking, may respond better to Lachesis. Those who respond well to this remedy are sensitive, nocturnal, creative people who move easily and quickly from the highs of creativity to the lows of feeling blue.

Temporary feelings of anxiety and feeling unable to meet unrealistic goals at work may benefit from Arsenicum album. Choice of this remedy would be confirmed by digestive upsets such as diarrhoea or nausea that are linked to anxiety, difficulty sleeping after the early hours of the morning and a general state of restlessness and dissatisfaction. All symptoms tend to be worse at night, while they all improve as a result of contact with sympathetic company.

Long-term action

Nutritional approaches

Re-vamp your diet, making sure that you give priority to foods that are as close to their unrefined, natural state as possible. In other words, avoid foods that have been preserved, tinned, refined, freeze-dried, dehydrated, or irradiated, since these items tend to have a considerably reduced nutritional value. If we make them the mainstay of our diet, we may find that we are less likely to fulfil our mental, emotional and physical potential. Instead, opt for a high proportion of raw foods in the diet, including fresh fruit and vegetables, cooked whole grains and cereals, steamed or stir-fried vegetables, live yoghurt, pulses and small portions of free-range dairy products. Also give priority to drinking four or five large glasses of still mineral water during the day – something that becomes an even higher priority when you are setting about cleansing your system after an excess of junk food, coffee, alcohol or cigarettes.

If you are going through a tough period of emotional and physical strain, make sure that you have enough foods in your diet to give you the necessary amount of B vitamins, since they play an essential role in maintaining the health and resilience of our nervous systems. Items that are rich in B vitamins include whole grains, nuts, fish, green leafy vegetables and products made from yeast extract.

Mood-balancing exercise

If you have a tendency to become irritable when stressed, or feel down pre-menstrually, you will probably benefit greatly from taking regular exercise. Aerobic activity that conditions our heart and lungs plays a significant role not just in boosting our levels of energy, but also in helping us achieve a greater sense of emotional well-being and stability. This is because regular aerobic exercise stimulates the production of endorphins in the body (these can be regarded as the body's own anti-depressants). It is the increased secretion of these chemicals that is thought to produce the natural 'high' that follows an aerobic work-out. It is most important to aim for regularity in exercising in order to gain maximum mood-balancing benefit from the activity, and to make sure that we are not overly-ambitious when we set goals for ourselves. Aim for half an hour of aerobic activity three or four times a week and always make sure that the exercise you choose is fun and appealing to you. Possible choices include brisk walking, cycling, low-impact aerobics, trampolining, or dancing.

Short-term fatigue

Even the best of us can suddenly hit a point during the day when we just feel it's a huge effort to keep going, and all we want to do is close our eyes and rest. If this feeling hits us at home where we have the space to take advantage of a quick nap, we may be able to do exactly this, but it just isn't possible when we are expected to be up to the mark at work.

Taking action: immediate measures

Breathing for balance

If we suddenly feel muzzy-headed and sleepy, we may be surprised to learn that we can improve the situation by doing something as basic as breathing more deliberately and consciously. Breathing is such an unconscious activity that we tend to disregard its significance in contributing to our state of mind and mood.

Not only does the process of breathing supply us with vital oxygen that we need to stay alive, but it also plays a vital role in removing toxic waste from our systems when we exhale. On the other hand, if we do not breathe to our maximum capacity, we take in less oxygen than we require, and we are also inclined to expel less toxic waste than we need to cleanse our systems. The unfortunate result can include feeling anxious, tense, sleepy, or sluggish and thick-headed. If you suspect poor breathing technique is contributing to feeling sleepy, try the following technique which is called alternate nostril breathing.

Bend the middle three fingers into the palm of the right hand, leaving the little finger and thumb extended. Place your thumb on your right nostril and breathe in through your left nostril for a count of four. Close both airways by placing your little finger on your left nostril, holding your breath for a count of four, before exhaling through your right nostril for the same count. Pause for a few seconds before repeating the cycle, beginning with the side you have just exhaled from. This process may be repeated four times on each side to clear the mind, and energise and refresh the body. Don't be put off if you work in an open plan office and feel embarrassed about being seen; just take a loo break where you can practise the technique in private.

Aromatherapy oils

A drop or two of any of the following invigorating essential oils may be inhaled from a handkerchief, or vaporised in a custom-made essential oil burner in order to clear the head and invigorate the mind: eucalyptus, grapefruit, rosemary, or peppermint.

Herbal help

A stimulating tea can be simply made by adding half a teaspoonful of finely grated fresh ginger root to a cup of warm water. Add clear honey to taste for a pleasant, warming, stimulating drink that also does wonders for the digestive system.

Eye exercises

If you feel that your eyes are heavy, strained or generally contributing to feeling sleepy and tired through overwork, try a simple technique called 'palming' the eyes. This can be done by closing your eyes and gently placing the cupped palms of your hands over your eye sockets. Keep the palms in this position for a minute or so, gently pressing them against the eye area while you breathe rhythmically and gently from your abdomen.

Neck rolls

If we feel sleepy and sluggish at work, we can benefit greatly from loosening up our neck and shoulder muscles. These are the areas where we hold a great deal of tension and tightness, with the result that circulation to the head can be less than efficient. Start by relaxing your jaw and loosening your shoulders so that they drop down an inch or so (a tightly clenched jaw and raised shoulders are a sure sign of tension being held around the neck and head). Drop your head gently forwards so that your chin is tilted towards your chest, slowly guiding the head towards the right shoulder. Let the weight of the head take it to rest as far back as it will easily go, circling it slowly and smoothly towards your left shoulder until it comes forward again. Breathe slowly and deeply and repeat the same movement on the left side, making sure that you do not force or jerk the head. These head rolls can be done twice or three times on each side, in order to fully relax the head and neck muscles.

Blink away strain

For those of us who work for long hours at VDU screens, or who have to spend extended periods of time reading documents, it is extremely important to remember to blink at regular intervals. Staring for a long time and forgetting to blink can make our eyes feel strained and dry; blinking at regular intervals provides essential lubrication for our eyes. Take some of the strain out of the eye area by closing the eyes for a second or two while resting the jaw, neck and shoulder muscles.

Further Reading

General titles

Chaitow, Leon, *Clear Body, Clear Mind: How to be Healthy in a Polluted World*, Thorsons, 1990

Fairley, Josephine, and Stacey, Sarah, *Feel Fabulous Forever*, Kyle Cathie, 1998

Helvin, Marie, *Bodypure*, Headline, 1995

Jones, Dr Hilary, *Doctor, What's the Alternative?* Hodder & Stoughton, 1998

Kenton, Leslie, *Endless Energy: For Women on the Move*, Vermillion, 1993

Kenton, Leslie, *Journey to Freedom*, Thorsons, 1998

Kenton, Leslie, *Ten Steps to a New You; A Complete Guide to Revitalising Yourself*, Ebury Press, 1998

Lavery, Sheila, *The Healing Power of Sleep: How to Achieve Restorative Sleep Naturally*, Gaia, 1997

MacEoin, Beth, *Healthy by Nature: A Woman's Guide to Health and Vitality in a Stressful World*, Thorsons, 1994

Weil, Andrew, *Eight Weeks to Optimum Health*, Warner, 1997

Wills, Judith, *Take Off Ten Years in Ten Weeks*, Quadrille, 1997

Alternative medicine

Fulder, Steve, *How to be a Healthy Patient*, Headway, 1991

MacEoin, Beth, *Natural Medicine: A Practical Guide to Family Health*, Bloomsbury, 1999

MacEoin, Beth, *Practical Homoeopathy: A Complete Guide to Home Treatment*, Bloomsbury, 1997

Peters, Dr David, and Woodham, Anne, *Encyclopaedia of Complementary Medicine*, Dorling Kindersley, 1997

Westcott, Patsy, *Alternative Health Care for Women*, Thorsons, 1987

Wildwood, Chrissie, *Bloomsbury Encyclopaedia of Aromatherapy*, Bloomsbury, 1996

Nutrition

Anderson, Luke, *Genetic Engineering, Food, and our Environment: A Brief Guide*, Green Books, 1999

Earle, Liz, *ACE Plan: The Secrets of Living Younger Longer*, Boxtree, 1993

Holford, Patrick, *One Hundred Per Cent Health: The Drug Free Guide to Feeling Better, Living Longer, and Staying Free of Disease*, Piatkus, 1998

Holford, Patrick, *Optimum Nutrition Workbook: All the Facts you Need to Know for a Healthy Life*, ION Press, 1992

Scrivner, Jayne, *Detox Yourself*, Piatkus, 1998

Personal development and relaxation

Benson, Herbert, *Beyond the Relaxation Response*, Collins, 1984

Benson, Herbert, *The Relaxation Response*, Collins, 1985

Chaitow, Leon, *Your Complete Stress-Proofing Programme*, Thorsons, 1985

Horn, Sandra, *Modern Techniques for Stress Management*, Thorsons, 1986

Jeffers, Susan, *Feel the Fear and Do It Anyway*, Arrow, 1991

Kenton, Leslie, *The Ten Day De-stress Plan: Make Stress Work for You*, Random House, 1994

Kirsta, Alix, *The Book of Stress Survival: How to Relax and Live Positively*, Gaia, 1986

Peck, M. Scott, *The Road Less Travelled*, Arrow, 1990

Wilson, Paul, *Calm at Work*, Penguin, 1998

Exercise

Baker, Sarah, *The Alexander Technique: The Revolutionary Way to Use Your Body for Total Energy*, Bantam, 1981

Barlow, Wilfred, *The Alexander Principle*, Arrow, 1984

Chuen, Master Lam Kam, *The Way of Energy*, Gaia, 1991

Lalvani, Vimla, *Yogacise*, Hamlyn, 1994

Marshall, Lynn, *Keep Up with Yoga*, Ward Lock, 1986

Marshall, Lynn, *Wake Up to Yoga*, Ward Lock, 1988

O'Brian, Paddy, *A Gentler Strength: The Yoga Book for Women*, Thorsons, 1991

Useful Addresses

General

British Complementary Medical Association
249 Fosse Road
Leicester
LE3 1AE
Telephone: 0116 282 5511

Council for Complementary and Alternative Medicine
Park House
206–208 Latimer Road
London
W10 6RE
Telephone: 020 8968 3862

Regulatory and advisory bodies

British Acupuncture Council
Park House
206–208 Latimer Road
London
W10 6RE
Telephone 020 8964 0222

Aromatherapy Organisations Council
PO Box 355
Croydon
CR9 2QP
Telephone: 020 8251 7912

British Association for Autogenic Training and Therapy
Royal London Homeopathic Hospital
Great Ormond Street
London
WC1N 3HR

Chinese Herbal Medicine
Register of Chinese Herbal Medicine
PO Box 400
Wembley
Middlesex
HA9 9NZ
Telephone: 020 7224 0883

British Chiropractic Association
Equity House
29 Whitley Street
Reading
RG1 1QB
Telephone: 0118 950 5950

The Society of Homoeopaths
4a Artizan Road
Northampton
NN1 4HU
Telephone 01604 621400

British Massage Therapy Council
78 Meadow Street
Preston
PR1 1TS
Telephone: 01772 881063

National Institute of Medical Herbalists
56 Longbrook Street
Exeter
EX4 6AH
Telephone: 01392 426022

Osteopathic Information Service
Osteopathy House
176 Tower Bridge Road
London
SE1 3LU
Telephone: 020 7357 6655

Exercise

Society of Teachers of the Alexander Technique
20 London House
266 Fulham Road
London
SW10 9EL
Telephone: 020 7351 0828

Parenting, pregnancy and childcare

Maternity Alliance
45 Beech Street
London
EC2P 2LX
Tel: 020 7588 8583

Maternity Alliance gives advice on the legal rights of parents, parents-to-be and mothers and fathers in the first year of their child's life. Contact their helpline on the listed number.

Home-Start UK
2 Salisbury Road
Leicester
LE1 7QR
Helpline: 0116 2339955

Home-Start schemes help parents of children under five who feel under pressure. They offer befriending and support, friendship and practical help to parents and children in their own homes. Contact on the number above.

Parentline UK
3rd Floor
Chapel House
18 Hatton Place
London
EC1N 8RU
Freephone helpline: 0808 8002222

Parentline provides support and help by telephone to anyone concerned about a childcare issue, especially where a parent feels under pressure. Call on the number listed above.

Index

self-defence plan, immune system and
   44–63
self-esteem 28
self-perception 28
shallow frying, as optimum cooking
   method 81
short-term fatigue 181–4
skin-brushing techniques, immune
   system and 51–2
sleep
   energising 22–4
   recurrent infections and 169–70
Slippery Elm, stomach upsets and
   172–3
slump
   after-lunch 10–11
   after waking 12–13
   early-evening 11–12
   mid-morning 9–10
   tea-time 11
smoking 74–5
'so-so' foods 77
soothing teas, recurrent infections and
   168
spices, stomach upsets 173
steaming, as optimum cooking
   method 80
stimulating foods 23–4
stir-frying, as optimum cooking
   method 80
stomach upsets 171–5
stress
   diffusing by simple tricks 130–4
   eating habits and 133
   emotional 127–34
   exercise and 100–1, 133–4
   immune system and 43
   making time 132
   negative 128–30
supplements
   immune system and 44–9
   need for 49–50
surroundings, attention to organising
   131

T'ai chi ch'uan exercise system
   119–20
tea-time energy slump 11
tea tree oil 63

teas
   as energy draining 73
   fruit/herb 70
   herbal, and stomach upsets 173
   recurrent infections and 168
thought patterns, positive 26–8,
   139–47
   immune system and 50–1
time
   on fitness activity 108–9 (table)
   stress and 132
tonics, herbal 21–2
triggers
   of anxiety 149–50
   of burn out 155–6
   of insomnia 161
   of mood swings 176–7
   of recurrent infection 165–6
   of stomach upsets 172
'trouble-shooting' strategies,
   nutritional boosters 83–93

understanding
   of fear 140
   of guilt 143–4
   of immune system 40–3

vegetables, fresh/raw 68–9
vegetarianism, arguments over 86–9
virgin olive oil, cold pressed 69
vital energy stimulation 14–16
vitamin C
   immune system and 47–8
   recurrent infections and 166–7
vitamin E, immune system and 48–9
vitamin supplements 89–92

warm footbaths, insomnia and 163
warming up, exercise and 112–13
water 70–1
water therapy, stomach upsets and
   172
weight loss, exercise and 113–14
whole grains 69
wholemeal products 69
work strategies, burn out and 156

yoga, as exercise system 118–19